The Housing Market:
a comfortable place to jump off the end of the world

Joseph D. Reich

Fomite
Burlington, Vermont

Copyright 2012© by Joseph D. Reich

All rights reserved. No part of this book may be reproduced in any form or by any means without the prior written consent of the publisher, except in the case of brief quotations used in reviews and certain other noncommercial uses permitted by copyright law.

ISBN-13: 978-1-937677-37-4
Library of Congress Control Number: 2012954918

Fomite
58 Peru Street
Burlington, VT 05401
www.fomitepress.com

Prologue:

One day just escaped desperately into the deep trails to get away from it all and suddenly saw through the trees the image of those very strange familiar pristine perfectly mowed backyards, like a kid staggering home drunk and laughing out loud in the moment because it all suddenly makes sense to him and realizes it all means absolutely nothing at all; the dazed dead ends of loop-de-loop, figure-eight cul-de-sacs like some sort of pop-up Monopoly board, like one of those vivid nightmares where you know exactly where you are but deep down inside got no idea where you are, and couldn't feel more lonely and alone and further away from it all like an aerial view from heaven to hell, like a peephole from the prison to the distant glistening turrets of the kingdom and how absurd it all was, how he felt absolutely nothing at all and all in that one crucial surreal moment realized how much of his life he had wasted out there and how it just felt so much more in here like a home or how a home was supposed to feel, and not exactly sure where to go, the turns, the alcoves, what was around the corner or what he even cared was around the corner; to finally care what was around the corner, the wild untamed growth of the forest, the madness of the butterflies and brooks and bridges, not caring where he was going or where he was going to even end up, and that really meant the world, like the soul opened up at last finally alone where no one knows him and he knows no one, alas a place, a place, a place where he may eventually call and be at peace with his being...

They laugh at me because I am different.
I laugh at them because they are the same.

— Kurt Cobain

Know where's absurd
and then when you can
run as fast as you can
the opposite direction...

The two female librarians butt heads
earth awakens

and the first amphibian
crawls up onto shore...

Life these days seems like a love letter
scribbled on the back of hate mail

milk & cookies in jail...

Born in a pregnant pause...

Being eternally tugged by the ear
down the hall by some principal
and still cracking one-liners...

One long detention hall looking up at some broken clock...

Getting into a face to face confrontation with piano tutor...

Beating the psychiatrist at his own game...

As a kid so out there and rebellious
used to make prank phone calls
to friend's parents...

Christopher Columbus
with mixed emotions
on the Santa Maria...

A tourist bus of mixed nuts
completely straight-faced
with flat expressions
dead to the world
rolling through
the apocalypse...

A square dance with a view of the volcano which blew its top...

The light to the candelabra
of the prison of the widow goes on...

One could not imagine more loneliness
which burrows through the absurd
and fragile and hollow core
of the illusion of suburbs...

Waving back and forth between the neighbors
(these actors and strangers in a sane asylum)
is like dazed distant and defeated convicts
reaching out through the bars of a prison...

Like a get-together
of demented relatives
who will never get you
and love and hate you
for all the wrong reasons...

Like once hearing how—
"Alcoholics will always try to
make you a part of their problem"
(and will turn on you in the instant)
what it's like to live or try to coexist
in a place or system or illusion like this...

The suburbs is trying to prove and discover
what's been discovered and proven
over and over and over again...

Out here it's like they duel to see who can hide it
and keep up the illusion the best almost like that
great big empty hollow feeling he used to get
when instantly needing to take a shit feeling
so lost and alone and overwhelmed in some
magnificent library or eternal nausea when
out of duress or obligation pressured to
make out with a girl because that's
what his friends had made him
or were supposed to or socially
and culturally expected of you...

He thinks living in this culture where it
is just simply one-upping thy neighbor
what makes him feel so damn lonely
so deserted and abandoned is there's
not a single soul which is the least bit
clever having to explain the punchline
which is a nightmare of the worst kind...

How they don't seem particularly brave
just a bunch of slaves like those dudes
he used to try to get away from back
in the day when sniffing glue without
a creative thought as they'd rather even
(if choice or volition even comes into play)
follow the gossip and rumor of the masses
like that distorted game of telephone you
used to play as a kid and the last translation
always turns out to be so much different than
the original message and the person possibly
perhaps with very good intentions ends up
becoming socially and culturally scapegoated
when paradoxically ironically may have been
a very independent thinker looking to contribute
something positive and productive to culture which
clinically too is what you learned as mildly delusional
never having physically or cognitively left the boundaries
of their suburb. The weather man gets it wrong half
the time and makes a nice living. Guess it's all about
the presentation and how he has the ability to small
talk and schmooze in the most boring and obvious
of cookie-cutter manners yet luckily the seasons
will always keep on turning and changing no
matter any of his man-made predictions...

The 'absurd' thing about the gossip and rumor
is how the 'little people' will thrive and function
and the only way they remain connected to their
environment and culture, yet how can one really
call this an environment or culture when completely
lacking in any true sense of meaning, truth, purpose
or substance, and thus, in the long run, ironically,
inextricably, these citizens become slaves and victims
to their own distorted and delusional rhetoric, clueless
and conformist with a lack of independent language,
body language, thought pattern, and expressions...

What people out here go out of their way not to do
is everything they're desperately trying to prove
which is all they have not done
and will never ever really do...

Never despise yourself
for your passions.

That's exactly how they're
trying to make you feel...

Put a watch on the *neighborhood watch*
as their judgment and character at best
is very "suspect and suspicious" and open
to scrutiny if ever experienced populations
and cultures like this so full of scapegoating
and stigmatizing and displaced hostility and
mass hysteria (whose social and cultural history
so crude and vulgar like a terrible family dysfunction
or abusive cycle of active-enmity and aggression
and even will appear to function and thrive off it)
the 'common' trait and characteristic
of the homogenized homo-sapien
of supposed advanced intellectual
cognition but when it really
comes down to it to instinct
and intuition and insight
and independent thinking
are insular and ignorant
(paranoid and defensive)
cookie-cutter, coward, clueless
and can never ever be considered
a 'real' culture if thriving off gossip
and rumor (self-generated myth
and mechanism of fear and hatred)
lacking in any true sense or for that
matter style of kindness and compassion.
When you really get close to them these people
(these empty and soulless specimens) are disgusting
(with their efforts) and will try to turn everyone (good
and caring and thoughtful individual) into a stranger
forcing them to question their identity and self-worth
and self-esteem and place and purpose in modern day
society of which can be easily 'forgotten' as so simply
(and simplistically) repetitive and obvious but not quite
as easy when talking about the principle and concept
of 'forgiveness' as so deliberate and conscious in their
pattern to inflict hurt and pain and malice and damage...

He used to thrive off brainwash on the back of cereal boxes
with their perfect 'well-balanced breakfasts' which showed
that bowl of cereal and marshmallows that were *magically
delicious* a piece of white toast with a slab of margarine
and a glass of orange juice and this was supposed to be
something like the well-balanced breakfast and thought
if he ate that and somehow was able to capture that
perfect fleshed-out scenario with the businessman
father in his suit and mom with the long dress
serving everyone with a grin in sun-drenched
pastel kitchen and ate that cereal with the toast
and the margarine and the glass of orange juice
would end up becoming the perfect citizen and be
just as happy as that family on the back of that box
of cereal. Somehow though he ended up spending a
hell of a lot of downtime in detention hall trying to talk
his way out of crazy things he had done like maybe one
of those forgotten figures at the bottom of a box of cereal...

He goes out into the woods which surround the circumference
of the cul-de-sac of homes and suddenly looks through the
trees over the farms and graveyards and stonewalls and
backyards and it all feels so strange and surreal as if he
doesn't and never ever belonged and feels so distant and
numb and even hostile and resentful in what all these
neighbors and monsters and automatons have taken
from him with their petty battles and wars and how
here in nature being solitary and alone feels
so much more familiar and at home...

He drives past every perfectly plush and primped-up lawn and can't help but to giggle to himself not because he wants to but because he has to and this is what he is eventually forced to knows every story behind every window all the bullshit and betrayals and just bad behavior on a daily basis the attempted suicides all the scars and secrets kept inside the losers who live by the lie and never apologize those who supposedly are supposed to be grownups and literally still don't know how to compromise to communicate so thrive off ignorance and hate and have monu/mental mini-meltdowns and don't return phone calls the know-it-alls who try and win it all obsessively on hands and knees to overcompensate and try to desperately convince others and somehow themselves with diesel motors and goggles and bad marriages; the alcoholism and the cheating on the wives; the convenient disconnect that they live by and then try to bribe by the going inside the ground for the pool a couple poodles or a cruise a really poor excuse to continue the collective brainwash and abuse...

When he goes down the dead end they're all polishing
up their lawnmowers with their bald gleaming heads
and big dumb proud lying smiles as you know every
single story behind them and how all their sons
resent them; Republicans who used to be Dead
Heads and now follow them around the house
with a whole list of chores they still owe them
(like 40 acres and a mule) and all end up either
joining the military or literally trying to kill
themselves just to get away from them and
if they talk back or perhaps happen to use
a bad word just to get them off their back
or express their frustration the stepmother who
he got for a steal is mandated to call the cops on
them (like some set-up structured system or agenda
or *treatment plan*) and they all eventually take off like
fleeing from some narrow-minded subjugating queen
and religion and most necessary Manifest Destiny to
either Reno or Denver to make names for themselves...

Always got to be doing something on the lollipop cul-de-sac.
Just can't seem to leave well enough alone nor quite feel
comfy or comfortable if they're not renovating or expanding
or building something up purchasing the new popular breed
or hybrid of dog buying a boat barbecue babysitter repaving
driveways putting in porches pools repainting homes; The
season is summer and thinks they're putting up a skyscraper
at the end of the dead end as keep on seeing the flatbeds
coming in purring like a load of loose women with
their ladders and lumber and Lego-like laborers...

How much more he prefers the wild dogs of the woods
than any of these trained dumb and domestic animals
on a leash going through their obsessive routines
and rituals on their front lawns to try and get on
ironically at the same time trying to prove they
belong; to desperately try and prove they are so
much better with the perverse psychological
phenomena of wanting to be worshiped
yet also absurdly pretending to warn

All seem scared looking over their shoulder...

The worst thing in being around them
around the liars and the fake wheeler
and dealers is you know all their games
you know their stunts before they're even
about to pull them and can always predict
it a couple steps ahead and it is never the
substance just an insult of the intelligence
as it's their intelligence which is the actual
insult and know every one of their games
ever one of their stunts before they know
it and before they're gonna pull them and
just a repeat of patterns of really poor and
weak character and behavior other words
translated (through hardcore experience
and observation and perception) wisdom

Nothing or no breed makes one feel more lonely…

He feels a strange comfort and solace in going out in these
woods which he cannot quite explain and wouldn't want
to and ironically instinctively has never gotten lost but
desperately feels that feeling or phenomena in this absurd
and obsessive prison of a pissed-off pristine cul-de-sac where
all of the neighbors real-life nightmares are just trying to one-
up each other and turn their grass into carpet until it's not
even grass anymore a kind of deep velvety shag rug as they
meticulously even if they have to maliciously keep their
eye out on it on him on you along with the weather from
the night before like the Indian teaching the white man
how to plant the first corn and of course never being
thankful and (still) not showing an ounce of gratitude
turning it into a paint-by-number picture postcard of
which the pod people are perversely not very welcoming
or kind and not coincidentally (obviously historically) try
to turn everyone into 'strangers' to keep their vision alive
while want to be worshiped and continue all the insular
delusions and lies, and inside nothing is moved or budged
an inch out of place and treated like a museum by the little
self-proclaimed control freak dictator curator and his slave
offspring procreator. They thrive by the disconnect and loathe
and hate you and will even try to get rid of you (annihilate
you) if you remind them of anything having to do with the
truth causing them to have to make some sort of connection...

Going into those rainy trails today he thinks how good
the rain feels, its distant yet very familiar trickling echoes
protected by the tall and tenebrous trees and pungent leaves
this being the only thing he will smell and see, the over-
flowing rambling roaring rivers surging beneath bridges
no tourists, no women walking clubs, no fucked-up Elmer Fudd
hunters shooting off their rounds and rounds of ammunition
in the distance, and thank the lord, holy and healing, knows
nobody will be there except for him and his lonesome being...

Out in the woods after all the rain and the strange change
of seasons the magical butterflies just naturally materialize
and decides he will simply follow them for as far as they
will take him out to a place in his fantasy world also
very grounded in the real world he may call home...

He dreams of one of those faux log cabins
in the paint-by-number wilderness where
he may finally miraculously be left alone
where people may finally mind their own...

Got so much more living left not to do...

Thinks to himself, long-gone, woebegone—

I want them to throw a surprise party at my funeral
At the surprise party I want there to be a murder
Life out here just way too freaking predictable

Know a good place to
get sushi? Calamari?
Thai? Heroine?

The fishermen come in...

The hero or rather loner who doesn't rely solely on poses
and can't afford to take it all for granted just eventually
gets real bored with all the pussy alpha-males; their
fake stoic and soulless roles and stapled-on goatees
and perfectly placed tattoos and cold and cruel looks
like they're still in Junior High School who he's got
to put in their place on a daily basis and leaves them
like a bunch of displaced *Starsky & Hutch* partners
muttering to themselves in their All-American
dominating King of the Road pickups

Not surprising how they appear
to have a shit load of self-disgust…

After spending full days in these soulless tourist towns
of cookie-cutter white devil Caucasians, incomplete
and fragmented, trying desperately to project roles
of arrogance and ignorance, attempting to give
the illusion of confidence and confrontation
never ever quite seeming to back themselves
up he realizes they're all just a bunch of
mounds and mounds of miserable
filthy and vulgar fleshy flesh

Landing the helicopters & motorcycles
& ferries & discos & circus & mulch
& lawnmowing equipment

(*Attention-seeker seeks attention-seeker
to act all indifferent and dismissive...*)

Misses the days of Clint Eastwood
who cut through all that pussy shit
with a simple squint and simply
fucked them up out of self-defense
not too far off the coast of Alcatraz...

He eventually dreams of gobbling up some Chinese feast
in the early evening of the suburbs just outside the ghetto
like a solitary Earlybird Special where nobody knows him...

Today just driving around
for no particular reason
maybe just trying
to escape the freaken
ridiculous homeowner's
association his wife
happens to mention
upon observation
about how some house
contains a certain amount
of stillness and says "Wow
baby that just seems to say
it all, doesn't it? Couldn't
have said it better" in truth
knowing deep down inside
that that's what been trying
to find his whole damn life

How always been kind
and never took that class
where they taught you to lie...

He swears he never ever really cared about *fitting in*
just the real nature and culture and civilization
(of its streets & ruins) & its women.
It's funny these adults or grownups
he thinks that's what you call them
(or what they like to be called)
appear so obsessed and will
religiously do whatever they
can to fit in and will even
go out of their way to
desperately try to prove
they fit in by actually
attempting to alienate
or humiliate someone
they believe is infringing
in on their self-entitled 'territory.'
If you ever get close or spend enough
time around these absurd and pathetic
and weak soulless organisms (the system
in which they live and how they function)
you eventually realize how filthy and vulgar
are these specimens like you ever even cared
for that matter in the first place to fit in where
you do get the absurd psychological phenomenon
of the true-blue 'theater of the absurd' trying everything
humanly possible to keep their very fragile and actual
delusional existences (of denial and fear) their 'keeping
up of appearances' (all of their repressions and obsessions)
whether it is the owning and controlling of their property,
their supposed community (which paradoxically don't
ever really contribute anything nice or kind or spiritually
but just keep on greedily taking and thinking the actual
'natives' are there just to serve them) and self-entitled
deemed territory or their own personal smug and arrogant
aerobic health club appearances of which they always give
way too much credence and significance, and even be as
superficial and shallow as to try and make a connection
or conclusion about others and project their own morals
and ethics onto them if they don't appear or resemble
them, and last but not least all the other things they

believe they equally control (or have some right to control) which includes the kids and the lawn mowing equipment and *the misses*...

He always wished for there just to be some parallel world
to a parallel world to a parallel world to a parallel world
just to make sure, as can't possibly imagine there being
anything more dull than what they got down here, some
stripmall of the soul and it's true it's the repetition which
kills you, gets you in the end (which literally dulls your
physical senses and causes you to lose your mental and
spiritual motivation and inspiration) these cultural codes
and societal roles, shallow and superficial systems and
materialistic items we worship and can't seem to exist
or live without (the absurd and pathetic *grownup* world
of reaction-formation and passive-aggression and over-
compensation) the horrible empty and awful nondescript
disconnect like a real-life nightmare like a gun to the head
(this ridiculous 'repetitive and redundant' non-architectural
soulless topographical landscape and lay of the land which
causes an excruciating situational depression as if America
all for the sake of progress filled up everything holy, sacred
with cement) a disconnect from the collective unconscious
yet so bad (and at such a loss) not even collective and not
even unconscious but painfully distorted and hyperconscious
and finds himself saying to himself my god this can't be what
the original statesmen had in mind and planned? Out here
has apparently become the opposite of freedom of speech
when people don't even realize they got free will and volition
and so busy and obsessed and fixated looking down at their
cellphones or ipads or whatever the fuck you call them? Will
even neglect their little children and not keep an eye on them
at the playground and when they fall and practically get
beheaded will make them feel guilty and lecture and yell
at them and make them wail all over again providing
them a nice dose of abuse and anger and Munchausen

Do independent thinkers even exist anymore out here when
such a mediocre and conformist and pathetic brutish look-
alike way of life and functioning becomes the norm, absurdly
glamorized and turns to the self-important and self-absorbed
(like swear to god never had some sort of father figure or
mentor) and have become slaves to their contraptions and
gimmicks? (He finds himself dazed and desperate in a land

of automatons caught somewhere between a headache and
nausea) returns home feeling like a melancholic monster
for never having caught on and being the sole survivor...

The real and true artist will always live in conflict
between civilization and the brutish hierarchy
of its actual *legal system* and all the people
which he threatens and what they project
on to him by their paranoid and defensive
nature and everything he represents to them
which is their freedom or more accurately stated
lack of freedom and all the freedoms which have
inextricably been taken away from them often by
their own basic and fundamental intrinsic single-
minded greed and selfishness, as well as what
they could not possibly even consider or conceive
by his natural and charming and clever and good-
natured character in really being a (far more) positive
and productive and contributing member of culture and
civilization and how often these delusional and brainwashed
individuals and society as a whole absurdly get this mixed-up
and backwards and take all their hostility and aggression out
on him due to their own selfsame denial and everything he
represents to them. The artist thus and then in the long run
will be alienated and treated as if he is invisible and does
not exist at all and 'The Eternal Stranger' and always live
in conflict between culture (and how it brutishly functions
by means of subjugation) and its hypocritical and contradictory citizens and what he eventually subconsciously and
consciously knows and feels from repetitive patterns and
experience by this rather cruel and brutal repulsive
collective character or behavior...

He thinks:

Sometimes it just feels like God
is taking one real long cigarette break
and if that be the case and not blaming
how much longer gotta wait for goodness sake
probably why everything feels like one long drag

And if talk about having the patience of a saint
I must have more than all of them put together
holed-up in one of those sanctuaries when you
gotta escape and just get outa the big bad city

Jesus asking if they got any rooms left
open at the inn when a marquee
clearly eternally reads *Vacancy*

You only really know and understand any
of these things after being consistently
betrayed and a feeling of not belonging

Trust me and mind and heart and soul set wandering...

He always found it so much more worse what they represent
(all those triggers and attributes to the raw core of emptiness
and unknown like a literal mythology suddenly come to life
of devastating feelings and emotions; the fable and parable
with its lethal fangs engulfing and swallowing the innocent
romantic protagonist when all he was ever doing was minding
his own business and turning him into a victim) than the
original trauma and experience (or repetitive patterns) which
may have actually caused them; Funny how from a phenom-
ological point of view, the opposite so often appears to
happen when dealing with the olfactory senses almost
like the dichotomy and difference between all things
cognitive and intellectual and visceral and imagined...

Out here he thinks they are so literal
and rigid and defined and definitional
and obsessed with following directions

almost as if they were doing something
holy and sacred. He could never take this
(or them) very serious and always found this

for the dumb and stupid; how they appeared
to absurdly and blindly abide by it and
couldn't help but mock and ridicule it.

Likewise and not too coincidentally
he was never very good at following
instructions and ironically always labeled...

His wife criticizes him for his criticism
(his survival and coping mechanisms
which she views as a lack of ambition)...

She says that he doesn't
know how to handle money.
This touches on her mortality...

Everything touches on his mortality
probably why he doesn't know
how to handle money...

He retorts that I moved us out here to give you a better life...

He can't imagine a worse life
as there is no real sign of life...

He tells her all in good fun--"Hey baby, maybe they got a cough medicine for your arrested stage of development!" She looks at the label and goes--"Look it's good for adults and children…"

Guilt is folded clothes
in the laundry basket
by the foyer window
in the evening drizzle
with tree frogs chirping
all around his home
lying himself down
next to her in bed
with his jeans
and t-shirt
and dirty
tennis
sneakers
still on...

This morning doing a lot of talking and being silly
she tells him she's overcompensating because
she has to go back into the mental health clinic.

He tells her he completely understands
and wonders how much of their lives
they spend in overcompensating.

Cracks window open
to let in a little sanity
wind chimes drizzle...

Where he now tutors just over The Bourne Bridge which
traverses the Cape Cod Canal which got built some time
in The Early Thirties to let the ships in and out, separating
Buzzard's Bay and the beginning of The Cape right around
the cranberry bogs over there at the Bourne Middle School
all the young teachers flirt with him and allows himself
to feel flattered like he's one of those bad boy studs from
another town who is forbidden; the teacher's assistants,
the detention hall monitor, the adjustment counselor,
those secretaries with the great big Botero bubble butts,
who probably shouldn't be wearing such tight slacks
to show off their Rubenesque contours, but do anyway;
Any which way it makes him feel good and apparently
makes them feel good and thinks of them when he's
traveling back home at dusk past *The International
House of Pancakes* on the rotary just before about
to head back over the bridge down the highway home...

There's that old man who always just hangs over the overhang
on his way out to Bourne and seems content in just hanging
out in the middle of the nowhere and the nothingness
of muted racing cars and swamps and cranberry bogs
and colonial inns set back in the forest and feels like
he's got so much more in common with him than anything
or anyone else out here and really does and stays with him
down the road until he reaches his fellow slurring mentors
who are grownup sisters and pretty nice people who are
trying to teach mathematical principles and the kids appear
sympathetic and wise past their years while most likely on
some kind of opiate or chemical dependency problem where
strangely enough they got a lot of that out here and a tradition passed down with way too much time on their hands
but who knows maybe not yet have learned a lot from them
and seem like pretty decent sorts...

The wiggers hang out in the parking lot
banging their beats from their pickups
trying to look all suspicious and start
up as guess it's so dangerous out here
and really got to watch your back
amongst the convenience stores
and laundromats of Cape Cod...

In truth the cheerleaders control the town...

Somewhere between the very sane and the very stable
are the stables of the very sane kept in one of those
very quaint clean waspy neat and organized New
England towns on The Cape where the parents
belong to very exclusive tight-knit closed-knit
circles of squares who will stare and look scared
if they see anyone around there who doesn't resemble
them in features and expressions and dress code right
around truth or dare country clubs and their kids not
quite so lucky kept hidden under the rug kept secret
not to be spoken of little further down the highway
at some methadone clinic in the historic district of
New Bedford along the river where Herman Melville
used to push off for all his great action and adventures...

Most have been raised
by their maids and babysitters
some even their butlers and gardeners
they know better than their own fathers...

Promise to god has seen them far more criminal
on a personal level living in the suburbs on a daily
basis, as opposed to those who have decided to devote
their lives to a life of crime for reasons far more traumatic,
abusive, things they have seen and witnessed and
experienced, and have no other choice in very short
and long-lived lives but to be reactive and impulsive...

Feels how it's all kind of ironic
never could really stand those
who weren't quite honest
as compared to those
who he knew
were thieves
and hustlers...

He dreams of painting all the picket fences
black and just spray painting them "bigot"...

He likens Mcmansions with their awful and nauseating brick and pillars and facades and four car garages to the mirage of those musclemen at healthclubs doing all that slamming of barbells and grunting and hollering way too loud and trying desperately to be all domineering and controlling looking at themselves in the mirror but not particularly good looking or intimidating or ever really saying anything too interesting and usually more than likely ending up very lonely appearing to be getting into a constant showdown with their being...

America lives and dies by its appliances and if you are
not compliant to rules and regulations all the way from
childhood and adolescence don't stand perfectly straight
in line in the hall of your school let your lawn go just a
little in the association and on the dead end not a cog
and cunt of the conformist corporation may very well
all the way up to the age and phase and system of
retirement get viewed as looked at and ostracized
into the uh-oh unenviable classification of an outsider
one of those troublemakers someone suspicious and
may even get that (un)lucky label of *undesirable* what
they used to call back in the day one of those agitators
if I'm correct may have even called them sympathizers?

Success measured by how well you keep it in and hide it
by how well you keep up appearances behind the not so
warm welcoming walls of prejudice and picket fences...

Most people have no idea what class is
and wouldn't know it as have never crossed
its path or used much of it in their existence.
Those who think they do are like a bunch of
funny cartoons and with all their hypocrisies
and contradictions nothing further from the
truth. What's the opposite of generous?

All the snobs are sitting out in the sand dunes
with their easels and canvas and doing their exact
same paint-by-number pictures of the exact same
scene acting like they're not to be looked at or talked
to or to even be seen like you even give a flying or care
to as this is what the rich do with their extra bucks and
when they retire and take summer classes (attend all
those readings and lectures and philanthropic functions
to cover up what a bunch of phony and neglectful and
dismissive fucks they really were and this of course just
like everything else in their life will make up for their
emptiness and guilt and everyone they fucked who
they should have been most close and supportive of)
pretending to be all that and that they are contributing
something great to culture and then with their connections
and nepotism and yes men and yes women will set up
art shows in only places they can afford for their fellow
blowhards looking no more creative or original than any
corny and clichéd scenario which hangs in a motel room
and now are like some great artists after they have spent
a lifetime being exclusive and alienating others and
making them feel like they don't belong (and ironically in
the dunes on the seashore are still doing the exact same thing)
treating other people like shit but you know don't exactly think
so cause don't think people like Monet or Van Gogh ever really
would have had to act like that while all you were simply doing
was strolling and clearing your head just to try and avoid exact
people like that...

He reflects...

How they try to turn you into strangers
and strangely enough end up hating you
even more when they find they're incapable...

He reflects...

In America if you become great
they adore then stalk then arrest
then assassinate then barter your
bio backwards to the highest bidder
and put it all in perspective with a nice
little bow & ribbon wrapped around it
then finish in your home in your home
town in your home state and show
how it all started with such idealism
and innocence. In America the assassins
become just as famous as their victims
and you can see how quickly lickety-split
the present instantly turns to past tense.
After you're dead if you become really big
they'll give lectures and the rich (from their
Summer retreats) will show up pretending
to be intellectuals and only when you're
good and gone and buried six feet under
will you discover all about your symbolism
and what made you tick and function I never...

He reflects...

When they literally raise (grow and develop) a culture and race to be insular and arrogant and classless and cocky and overconfident what they're actually breeding is diseases...

Upon reflection he always sees the exact same kids in
detention hall who just can't seem to keep themselves
out of trouble and are regulars and can't help but to
rebel and so surreal with pained expressions and
wise ass smiles and his whole childhood just
comes naturally flooding back to him...

The sound of the afterschool *awkwardstraw* coming down the hall (with its strained tubas and horns) always sounds like some sort of muffled cacophonous pachyderm being put down. No one seems to ever notice it; the special needs teachers and the afterschool kids, as just becomes a part of the natural environment awkward growth & development...

He finds himself still turned on by all the older women
who flirt and come on to him; the adjustment counselors
and the mental health clinicians who apparently
see something in him but what is he gonna'
do and simply returns their favor...

Wants to spoon the substitute teacher...

He wonders why in America they always seem bent, hell bent
on obsessively teaching you your lesson or learn your lesson!
Learn your lesson! Learn your lesson! Learn your lesson!
Until this was all he heard like a broken record and rebelled
against it and was consistent at being the class clown and
cut-up and wise ass and naturally sarcastic and a staple
well known in the principal's office and detention (even got
to know all the monitors and secretaries and about their
families as well) of this he excelled and had absolutely no
regrets and in looking back probably the first time in his
life had no doubts or hesitance as in being all grown up
looking at all these people who are supposedly supposed
to represent grownups the ones who apparently learned
their lessons are still some of the biggest kiss asses and
phony and half-holy hypocrites you'd ever want to meet
or for that matter not want to meet and got nothing
to say and don't want to say a thing to them…

He thinks once again while driving down the highway home
that this country's just one big crooked cop trying to catch
you in a speed trap get his quota and paperwork done when
you're just trying to get home to see your loved one and where
this country has really gone wrong and down the drain (even
a little insane which is the worst kind of sane) is they no
longer really care about the care or support and guidance
you provide your clients nor provide any sort of support or
validation but more so all about paper work so they can
continue to get funded and units and re-upped and thus
the creepy crawler clones who actually get rewarded
in the long run are the most soulless and mechanical
the most tedious and trivial...

He develops an overactive libido
(for coping & survival reasons...)

And imagines the wives in compromising positions
who always put themselves in compromising positions...

They become a part of his dream fantasy and tries to extend them as long as he possibly can throughout the day...

They always wave at him and walk with very tight jeans
on right outside his window and poke their heads into
the woods bending over blatantly somewhere between
the real and unreal world almost trying to draw him
into their natural animal instincts and desires.

They haven't been touched by their husbands in awhile...

We naturally attach fantasy and image
to all those things which we may have
lost and has passed us (for no particular
reason or profound and traumatic almost
like the traits and features of an arrested
stage of development) in our existence

i.e. Dozing off to the natural cadence and rhythm
of the surf and can almost measure by our natural
senses how it comes in and builds up and crashes
onto shore then slowly slips back to the ocean like
the nature of an orgasm and climax and pillow talk

One of the few and only beautiful radiant forms of
repetition while these are some of our most keen
and perceptive senses and experiences as well as
a simple spare environment which is a practical return
to the innocence of our youth and adolescence and
remains forever etched in our transcendent consciousness...

He dreams of all of his true-blue Jewish Borderline girlfriends who were so clever and crazy and kind and how they would give him rimmings and foot massages and would do it like three to four times a night wondering how they were doing and their lives and if they were even still alive considering all the times they had tried and the drama inside and outside...

That borderline girlfriend who he used to love or thought what love was supposed to be with all the constant back and forth push and pulling mad and crazy histrionic drama how she used to in a flattering way say--'I do love you, you're just a little rough around the edges" and used to take that as a compliment and after they broke up for like the million and a half time and found someone who was even more charming and kind and halfway sane how he didn't trust this new one literally from that past relationship as upon reflection having developed a 'fear of intimacy' or just couldn't get used to her normalcy or the normalcy of things if things weren't mad and crazy and took at least a full year almost to redirect his brain back to a decent equilibrium (to something resembling a recovery) what made him really love her were the couple of kind words of support she told him "I think *she's* a little rough around the edges!" and in that one single moment took a great big deep breath and just started to think...

He broods...

How it's funny they look at you like a criminal
when yer at your most holy & sacred & paid
yer dues & down & out & beatific & when
yer in yer stupid health club shape sculpted
(a part of the herd masses & faux spiritual
& trying to project some sort of image)
going through all those grueling routines
& rituals & really actually quite unmotivated
& uninspired with existence & a slave to the system
like Jack Lalaine on heroine act like they want to fall
in love with you & marry you & want you to take care
of them & drop it all & throw it all away for you hmmm...

Go figure? The places we meet
the places we get separated...

Out here all it is about is compromise
act and talk a lot about compromise

They are actors and talkers of compromise
(nothing could be more nauseating)

Nothing could be
more of a lie...

Like some really fragile
and fucked-up version of Heaven.
No Hell could be any worse than this...

He thinks the way he's been feeling
can actually hear every last forest falling
every last tree while no one's around to hear it

(and still remains completely irrelevant)

Throw mama from the train a kiss
wonder how she feels about this
or just goes along for the ride...

One day just walked out his playroom
into the wind and dark and drizzle
down to tree frogs and never returned

What it means to be eaten up
by a green apple in the refrigerator...

Surviving off oranges
and iced coffee
dreams
suicidal
ideations
he thinks
wants to be
like the fish
in the fish bowl
when the lights
go down in his
kitchen and all
that's left is a
castle and blue gravel
and shadowy scenario
surviving off both
flashing t.v. in his
dark home and the moon
through the window sees himself
as both the protagonist and hero
savior and criminal in all those
late night film-noirs when he
was the only one around and
all alone following the trail
yet also being followed
on-the-run not so much
a clash of egos
more so a duel
between id
and superego
suppose both
Edward G. Robinson
and Orson Welles
with nowhere to go
searching for the trap
door in the stars above...

They always try to spook you with the whole fable and mythology of the eerie and invisible disappearing ghost and spirit; He thinks how much more he'd prefer seeing these motherfuckers simply disappearing! Man wouldn't that be the shit and never be seen from or heard from again and all those humble and self-effacing ghosts who never asked for fanfare would appear and assure you they'd have something so much more meaningful and substantial to say as well as appreciate the atmosphere and ambiance and not be such control freaks simply playing mind games half-crazed with their overcompensating and obsessive needs to be sane…

Lonely, lonely, lonely, lonely
could fill up one of those
high school flasks or
beakers with lonely
what was that called
volume? Misplaced
my mandolin, my
proof of being
why he drinks
warm coffee
at twilight
and listens
to sports radio
"Hey Tim
in Trenton
what's up?"

Some people do it with class
Some just doesn't...

Codependent meets codependent
dependent on codeine medicine
you pick up over the counter

"Just put it on our tab..."

Imagines the image of glue sniffing addict
who got his start putting together parts
of model ships and model airplanes

Like all those greats who got addicted
to painkiller to originally hope
to heal a little the pain...

He thinks back to almost every person he has ever looked up
to trusted and admired who has ironically and consistently
let him down in some obscure or quixotic form or another
and felt cheated or a certain sense of betrayal and looking
back felt pretty deeply devastated even empty and hollow
but now in retrospect pretty shallow as wisdom
now precludes just a bunch of fools and actors

He thinks always dug that song 'Man of Constant Sorrow'
in practically every version frontwards and backwards…

Sees umbrellas as serving multiple purposes
(as functional and decorative and for reasons
of escapism) as evidenced by the great old-time
slapstick comedians Dick Van Dyke and Winston
Churchill, Mary Poppins hittin' the silhouetted
rooftops of London, Humphrey Bogart and the
snickering Penguin with his sudden and out
of control onset diagnoses of Tourette's...

He thinks would it be too cliché to say I want to rest
my head in the belly of some insane farm girl with a
Southern drawl perhaps maybe Midwest right there on
the border and cry out my soul the history of the world
and when I'm good and gone she simply goes--"Joe, I'm
gonna go pick us up a six-pack and couple corndogs maybe
even a po'boy and clamroll!" and for the first time finally in
so damn long feels at home the scent of *Deep Woods* on him
like some fine cologne and compost already laid out in the
puddly cornfield where seagulls gather and then take off...

Thinks
about
those
boys
who
just
got sick
of the war
and decided
it wasn't
for them
anymore
and now
seem
pretty
damn
glad
just to
be back
in that
small town
with a grin
no strings
attached
pumping gas
in the rain
in a field
of corn...

It's really the kids who ring in the seasons
the whoosh of the wind and dogs barking
keep you sleeping just getting your flesh
and bones beneath the ocean the cherry
on the sundae; wonder what it was
like for those dudes the morning
they blasted off to the moon?

Brides waving good luck charms
bringing shit to the dry cleaner
and practicing their ball room
moves for when they returned

The state fares
have all taken off
leaving just the fables
the rabies of stray dog

Seductive girls
& delinquents
& a moon stranded
way up high up there
giving the impression
of some kind of home...

Ask the deep dark night
what it's like after
it rains at night?
Ask the bending pear
tree whose glistening
beaded silver branches
glow against bedroom window?
Turns out all those pen pals you had
were not particularly sincere or loyal
that editor who asked you to leave
the wife and kid you literally taught
the business and got her out of crisis
after crisis with her conflicts with
her husband, chasing utility men
around her kitchen with knives
and daughters trembling under
tables when the cops came
because they felt guilty
that they were the cause
of it all and providing her
clinical support how children
always take it on themselves
and to clearly explain to them
that it was not their fault
but now being the classy
self-admittedly borderline
bitch that she is guess
because didn't take
her up on her proposal
and leave the wife and kid
gonna now hold it against
you gonna hold onto it
until her hearts content
(has her heart ever been
content? will that exist?)
emotional blackmail
till the cold controlling
heart resists and keeps it
on the eternal waiting list
funny taught her all about
the business about contracts
as well and everything else
so ask the deep dark night

what it's like after
it rains at night
the bending pear
tree whose silver
glistening branches
glow by the side of
bedroom window...

Finally gets a little shut eye in the shower
after nights and nights of nightmares
and insomnia, like that moving scene
from that movie "King of New York" after
Christopher Walken just gets out of lockup...

He thinks he will go down with the tree frogs tonight...

These days peculiarly finds himself dreaming of his mother's
girlfriends when he was a kid for some odd reason perhaps
to take care of him while at the same time having longing
lovely long-lost loving suffering sex with them
the ones he perceives were good looking or
the hippies with the long black hair and big
bushes and long sundresses without bras on
could look down and never did and now does...

Man should learn to be more grateful
but only seems to be so after border
line girlfriend walks out on him for
no particular reason leaving him
high and dry with empty bed
syndrome and only really
knows after something
better comes along
with a pair of
purple panties
hanging off
doorknob...

The little bulb in the refrigerator goes out and he puts
the pickles back in from the night before pondering
on the pot in the morning in the half-bathroom
and cracks the window open a little to let in

The wind from the end of Winter from that great big farm
over the stone wall and wife's silk panties which sit in a
colorful bundle on the old chipped read antique chair
in the corner around the pumpkin candle which sits

On a little book of Monet's murals. The only thing
which ever seems to get his head screwed back on
is staring straight into the nightlight glowing in
the plug and wish-washing of the washing
machine to faraway places unknown...

Fish always swishes out from his castle
waving his fins and gills, long feathery

melancholy tail to self-soothing
flicker of hypnotic candle...

He watches in a hypnotic trance as well
'cause when it comes down to it there's

really nothing left to do and only
thing that makes any sense at all...

Spends the morning listening to lingering secretaries speak
(almost the opposite of Socrates in one long fluid breath but
loving every last second of it) while waiting for the wife
because of chronic back pain and seemed to say it all
all in like 15 minutes or so talking about *Papa Gino's*
and how she got all these buffalo wings for half price
and a pizza with pepperoni on it how she's not sure
if her boyfriend's gonna take her out to Niagara Falls
or Atlantic City over the weekend doesn't much matter
anyway all pretty much the same and the price of gas
and don't necessarily anymore need passports if in
the region but these things called passport cards and
the fog and dogs and all about the dogs just walking
the dog round and round the backyard and getting
some sort of new moisturizer as the other one completely
dried her face out but doesn't need to worry about it in
the Summer cause her face gets all oily and how she can't
conceive how people call up complaining about all this
back pain and then just never showing up and yeah
when you think about it just summed it all up just
seemed to say it all in like 10 or 15 minutes or so
and when we thanked them thanked them for
so much more all through that little window...

Hypothesizes a theory to heal the marriage problem divorce
problem in America to make the bond or the baseline just a
little more holier just a little bit stronger should be forced
to walk down the aisle once again the exact same crowd
staring at them the exact same season the exact same
ceremony the exact same people giving them away
the exact same weeping the exact same bridesmaids
the exact same bachelors trying to make moves on
bridesmaids the exact same drinking the exact same
toasts thrown the exact same flowers thrown the exact
same old timer throwing his back out the exact same first
dances the exact same last dances and then decide if they
really want to give up or make another go at it the exact same
presents and with the guilt money the gelt the loot take a nice
big deep breath and head out to the airport once again and
when they get to their destination when they open up their
suitcases when they examine the buffet when they take a nice
big deep breath and overlook some nice big deep ocean will
clearly know or not know and if not at least say that was
a pretty damn good ceremony a pretty damn good party
a pretty damn good Sunday a pretty damn good try
a pretty damn good life...

He remembers this kid he grew up with brilliant
mathematician smart Jewish kid turned out one fine
warm late Spring evening randomly robbing a pharmacy
at gunpoint (taking his chances not giving a fuck about
the full equation or even for that matter the solution) with
one of those weird freaky clear masks on way before they
got all cool and trendy and film-noire kind of blew his mind
and caught them all off guard as had no idea was that
hard and turned out he had had an addiction to painkiller
and remember in a very strange way earning mad respect
for him 'cause was independent and desperate and went at it
creative not bringing anyone along anyone down with him and
going completely so/lo as where they went to school they all
felt like a bunch of fucken followers and think without even
realizing it just got so sick of how they always used to
brag about its reputation and real competitive and it's
like they stole and didn't let you have a childhood and
didn't know he was so out there and had it in him and
what led him and tried to picture the image so of course
they took away his scholarship to college and for that
reason alone for that reason as well not giving a fuck
and fucking up his future couldn't help but love him...

They all grew up in these great big mansions. Had all the time in the world to prove their manhood. Become romantics. To make something of themselves and all the pressure to live up to unrealistic expectations. Never saw their parents. A whole system of privilege and entitlement and collective consciousness of how the rules just don't and will never apply to them. But ironic every last single one of them turned to drugs and drinking. Dropped all their close friends they grew up with to do these things. Cop it together. Cut and separate the lines together. Snort it all up together. This became what they believed made them creative (*higher than holy*, sacred) but didn't realize through these routines and rituals, repetitive and petty and pathetic, what actually made them conformist and just as guilty and often as full of contradictions as the things they were rebelling against. Went to the same burn-out parties together when the parents were at their second homes on the weekend. All slept with the same people. All teenagers who had already acquired closed circles. All went to the same group therapy for anger management which really stemmed from parental neglect. Father figure workaholics busy making names for themselves sculpting their very distinct reputations. *Dis stink* reputations. What stems from a very competitive school system. All used the same tutors and psychiatrists. They all grew up in these great big mansions...

He thinks tonight I saw one of the funniest things of all time
well not really but kind of; While walking on my treadmill
after all the local rape & murder & crumbling infrastructure
& just another Indian merchant getting robbed at gunpoint
on the corner, they reported about "A House Party" where
there was underage drinking and this very stern and serious
cop being interviewed speaking very sincerely about *public
intoxication* as well as *impairment* and thought wasn't that
what high school was all about wasn't that 'the best of times
wasn't that the worst of times' but there was some specific
clause in there something along the lines that they could not
be charged because the parents or thought I heard *social folk*
or some term or another weren't made aware or informed of
and just showed this perfect looking home with a perfectly
manicured lawn and three car garage and just like one
of those wild underage drinkers of public intoxication
and possible impairment couldn't help but laugh aloud
and think damn how times have changed how those
were the best of times those were the worst of times...

He thinks in growing up wish just once had done something
productive like fool around with one of his older sister's
girlfriends and just once be the talk of the town instead
of what they ended up talking about.

There *was* Jill Lawton this really hot older girl who was in the
grade just above him who said she liked both him and Terry
Bloom a good friend of his and tried to pit them against each
other and said if one of them had asked her out would give
them the honor of going out with her

And told him you can have her and ended up kind of like he
expected having to fight her so-called ex-boyfriend and saw
right through her and kind of saw this happening and had
a feeling she was still going out with him and felt at least
during that period of existence really not worth it

But thought good for Terry (and think was actually even
happy for him) able to make out with her in the woods by
the library and looking back thinking probably had the
attitude like he didn't give a shit as believe came from
a pretty broken family

Looking back at childhood it was all pretty damn
brutish and ridiculous and passionate and scary…

He thinks about we were friends as adolescents maybe even teenagers and that is all that really matters and came before all that madness all the meanness and coldness during that phase and *stage* of puberty of what it meant to be a young adult (all those bizarre broken promises and betrayals turning you into some sort of stranger out of nowhere) and will always stay in the transcendent consciousness imagination forever...

As a kid he actually did try to dig that hole to China
(and really believed) but somewhere along the way
just kind of gave up or lost interest and faith. This
he found very much to be the key metaphor for life
and tried it too for one of those *Tootsie Roll Pops*
how many licks would it take to get to the middle
guess very similar to digging that hole to China
and whole metaphor for life drama and trying
and then guess just somewhere down the line
sort of giving up or getting distracted or losing
direction and motivation or the whole aggressive
staying on right path self-righteous bullshit question...

He thinks he lives by metaphors.
If not for that out here he'd fall
for and become a victim to all
their brainwash and folklore...

He was always amazed (well not really
kind of tongue in cheek in a numb and keen
and instinctive kind of way) on this dead end
when he had first moved out here the people
they said were good neighbors or good fathers
(or some other form of inaccurate idiot dialogue
nepotism and brainwash as must have had a very
low baseline or ethical standards) and the ones who
had the alcohol problems and bad marriages as turns
out the latter he found out actually ironically were always
so much more down to earth and modest and humble and
sincere and loyal like those extended members of the family
you never ever really knew who they always said were really
nice and kind and turns out when you ran into them at bar-
mitzvahs and weddings and funerals in real life were some
of the biggest assholes and you were so much better and true
as you could only imagine what they were saying about you?

Often empirically within the family system of 'family
dysfunction' and the broken nuclear family unit one has
a very weak and fragile identity and ego and little to no lines
of communication and an individual (or group of individuals)
who simply are insecure and envious and jealous, and
through impulsive and reactive behavior will align and look
to find a victim; the critical, clinical (subjugated/symbolic)
scapegoat to project and dump and transfer and superimpose
all their self-loathing, hostility, and shortcoming weaknesses
and will do anything (humanly often inhumane) possible
to alienate (to humiliate and embarrass) him in order to
thrive and function (while the actual supposed elders or
leaders or role-models of the family do absolutely nothing
about it continuing to enable this behavior and vicious
cycle) and like that ridiculous, primitive, juvenile
game of telephone one used to play as a kid where
the message always got distorted and the innocent
turned victim is forced to take on that stigma or label
(whatever be their character or ethically make the effort
'to prove themselves') and all one can do is disengage or
physically and spiritually divorce themselves from the source
of the trigger, and refuse anymore to accept or take on the
inaccurate label of scapegoat and escape and to leave all
the goats whispering passing new gossip and rumors
in order to screw someone else up to survive and cope...

Boyhood felt as brutish and absurd as having to meet
for rumbles after school to protect some sort of shallow
and superficial code of honor which never seemed
particularly honorable of course no one showing up
to the battle and all the surreal and dramatic silly
side talk and prattle which preceded that of what
each side was gonna bring secretly gasping a
private sigh of relief which back then seemed
to touch on the whole notion and concept of
your being and mortality and fragile identity
and guess never amounting to a thing…

Seems a couple decades later when they're all supposed to be
grownups it hasn't changed much, a matter of fact, not at all
and far worse and just the same assholes who will literally thrive
(and it becomes a part of their language and body language)
by passing gossip and rumors giving away their weak and
fragile identity and character on the spot and more times
than not, how pathetic and empty and hollow
their 'domestic life' appears to be back home...

Even as far back as Junior High School it was fools the mediocre and the masses who appeared to act and function this way and for the rare individual found this 'beyond belief' and 'unbelievable'...

He thinks how all those word problems they forced on you
in Junior High School should have been more reality-based
and relevant and true asking you how long will it take you
before you lose it from a bunch of false and fake fools
of a supposed support system of flattery and reaction-
formation when all you can do is escape and act-out
and be on-the-run in Civ. 101 climbing up the pipes
of the cathedral on the corner of every city in America
when you come in on your Greyhound at dusk crawling
up that cross to the snowy stars of some seasonal smog

Midge sticking a needle in her arm...

He thinks when I go and defense-mechanisms can't stand up no mo' like some kid eyeballing the sun backwards through a magnifying glass fighting off the sun and then the smoke and then the flames I want them to stuff and can me in a can in one of those canneries shut down along some old haunted autumnal eternal constantly rolling river mill town in West Virginia or Pennsylvania even one of those heavenly dewy Northern states hidden nestled deep in the matchstick hills before you set foot and tippy toe and pirouette into Canada…

Today in his depression
he meandered like one of
those madmen through
the *Super Stop & Shop*
talking to himself and
laughing at his own
jokes always making
a nice connection with
the pretty Portuguese girls
behind the deli counter who
are literally like little sparkplugs
and dynamite looking and to die for
and only wish life and existence and
relationships could be like this picking
up 2 dwarf watermelons 4 comic books
for his kid and danish for his wife who
out of stress and anxiety has been vomiting
and having the runs and then deliberately
taking the scenic route through the ghetto
to lose himself and forget it all and return
home feels semi-heroic unloading the bags
and picks at the Greek pasta salad with
numb seedless brain and finally later on
that night at the bewitching hour with
the dwarf watermelon running down
his neck takes his first deep breath...

He thinks how she jogs from her mom's in the woods
over to his on the dead end on days that she is sure
that he'd be out there and would casually give her
a polite glance or throw out his hand then she'd
look down to the ground or way up in the air
leaving to make him feel like most guys end
up feeling like he was into her or after her
wanted a part of her and swear was just
mowing his long impossible lawn and
never really even thought (or thought
much) she had very much to offer
yet strangely enough continues
to put him on her route and
itinerary of things she's
gonna reject and try
to make feel lost
and awkward...

He's not sure what's worse
pictures left crooked on the wall
by too many slammed doors
or time and the seasons
and what life does?

He dreams of being squashed like the seeping colors
like the blood of the butterfly against his garage wall
like some ancient Indian painting which just says it all...

He dreams of receding and never being seen
from or heard from again into the ticking
of the clock of the lake twisting through
the trees of the lagoon of the midnight
mountains of the mansions of the moon...

When
he's had it
and fed up
with life
and blurts
out such
things like
Jesus Christ!
really some
where
under
there
is a little
prayer just
reaching out
just crying
out for help
somewhere
down there
deep down
inside…

He thinks Jesus should have just dressed in drag the night before and simply slipped out the door and how much better would be *The Greatest Story Ever Told* just vanishing into thin air to reunify once more with his father up in Heaven and say I give up on these people they just don't get it thinks by the nature of man and human nature when they have one of those celebrations they would have so much more respect for him as these mortals appear to appreciate more and respond better to natural consequences and Machiavelli's 'Is it better to be feared or loved?' And thinks too what a better world more in keeping with the spirit of a fugitive on-the-run than a martyr who was betrayed and done wrong...

He hears himself saying to his wife while waiting on the child pick-up line "I don't need to be saved, just want to be left the hell alone!" It's all said in good fun as she had casually mentioned "I've tried to do everything I can to save you" and with hand over hot throbbing head can hear the wind whipping through the wilderness and the creaking of the bending limbs like the squeaking swings of a jungle gym...

They both doze off to Bob Marley's—
"Lord I got to keep on moo-oving
where I can't be fou-und..."

He sees through his windshield while waiting
those young and beautiful mothers in their
tomboy tight jeans and long and lovely
silky black hair and sneakers go to
pick up their creatures blissful and
happy like one of those good old
silent black & white movies leaving
so much room for the imagination...

She's a good girl and Portuguese and beautiful
and works at a thermos manufacturing company
across from the elementary and every time around
3:30 when the bell rings when he's picking up his kid
sees her darling figure darting across that perfectly
green plush lawn of the thermos manufacturing
company still looking very young and pretty
an eager and concerned smile and those very
tight blue jeans on and perfect dandelion behind
crossing the road past the whipping American flags
and cardboard tulips in the windows to pick up and
meet up with her son lucky kid and if only he knew...

Another time waiting on the child pick-up line
to kill time will call up friends from way back
when but know they probably won't be around
anymore and long gone and a sad thought in itself
so tries not to think about it and simply solely their
moms and thinks why not and maybe get to know
them better ask which room they're sitting in how
life's been what's the weather but like everything
else decides not to as would probably be a real
let down or worst of all kind of neutral and decide
to leave it all behind for memories and imagination...

He thinks he wants to do a connect-the-dot
backwards to his origins as that might be
just as effective if not more sort of what
they try to teach the kids displaced and
living at group homes for when they get
angry and frustrated and feel alone and
to try and count backwards idiot shit
like that which never ever seems
to work probably why he decides
(or not) to ever pick up the phone...

He wishes just once would pick up
and magically pick up where they
left off as if time had never passed...

He views time as everything that got left
behind for no particular reason sort of like
the natural growth & development of evolution...

He views time as those mesmerizing
moments when creation met evolution...

Like the caterpillar to the cocoon
and the butterfly to the season...

Cognitive delay
in the eye of
the beholder...

Father will brainwash son and treat him like a possession
and literally with self-idolatry and adulation and bullshit
and manipulation (one may even view it as something of
a spiritual and psychological harassment) 'little man'
pretending desperately to be 'big man' actually have him
believing in his false and fake alarm obvious charm heroism
as boring and going through the motions as you can get like
one of those stick figure diagrams one would instantly forget
when in his heart of hearts is one of the biggest cowards and
kiss asses and followers to ever walk the face of the earth
a fine line between Nazism and religion and this type
of relationship of slavery/subjugation

Kid never had a fighting chance...

Blues or something so true: don't ever be afraid ever be
ashamed eagle flies overhead from the nowhere to some
where and doesn't care where it's going yet somehow
makes everything alright again cotton candy man ain't
got no more candy left to sell to the abandoned guests
so decides to just dance instead always got along so
much better with the wild roosters wandering the side
of the road the mothers and the kids and the wind

Almost there...

After all the craziness, the moods, the damage, the situational
depression in a situation he just can't seem to get himself
out of, his wife takes his son on a play date in the heart
of the decaying suburbs and he leaves her a simple
message on her cellphone like the remaining
ripples coming in off the ocean "Maybe
you want to teach Dylan how to swim.
Maybe you want to teach him to
swim in the above-ground pool."

He doesn't expect a return
phone call and that will do...

He weeps on a bench in Providence not knowing where to go...

Every day kid forgets his trumpet and every morning mother takes in his trumpet he forgets to bring in and this becomes something of a tradition and as if this had never happened she reminds the secretaries at the front desk he forgot his trumpet and can you give it to him and they casually grin and returns back home to wherever she goes wherever she is...

He imagines the crossing guard
with her uniform stripped off
and her right above him with
stop sign over his neck going—

Stop! Go! Stop! Go!
Stop! Go! Stop! Go!

Crow's nest just sitting solitary silhouetted way up on top the tippy-top of the treetop way above it all...

He feels as vulnerable and exposed and fragile as an egg and decides to just turn on the weather on the radio which gives him the strength the high and low tides on The Cape and the repeated weather report and gales and patterns and actual size of the waves out in Warwick, Rhode Island Providence, Narragansett by this eternal amorphous mechanical voice, and even though he doesn't know exactly what they're talking about it seems to just all make sense to him and may even somehow ground him...

He thinks all my failures have succeeded
at failing and don't take them too seriously
as not really sure how truly serious he was
about any of those things in the first place...

He thinks all those people
who always tried to get me
not to believe always made
my senses so much more keen
got me so much more to believe...

Watch how they try to break you
as for me it's never the big people
as they're just not a lot of people
who can do that to me and simply
all the little shit all that little repetitive
shit that just keeps on repeating itself
over and over and over again all that
ridiculous and absurd and petty
little pussy shit in between...

With bloodshot eyes he decides while driving through
do or die bland and barren land of suburbia (of artificial
intelligence/of melancholia) will erect a mailbox and paint
it black with either white letters or paint it white with just
black letters and it will simply say *God* and will walk back
and forth everyday knowing deep down inside there will be
nothing inside but just this simple exercise of walking back
and forth knowing in the back of his mind there'll be nothing
in there seeing the different traits and characteristics of the
seasons, the subtle colors, the varying smells and shadows
just his thoughts and emotions and reflections will mean
the world gonna paint a mailbox which just
says God with absolutely nothing inside...

Broods...

At the end of your life your greatest Hell will be your greatest Heaven when you used to play your burning guitar in your lonesome window in New Orleans thrust into self-imposed isolation when your silhouette became solitude and vice-versa surviving off Cornflakes and bananas dreaming of the corn fields of Iowa and your long lost beautiful blonde you missed so much somewhere in the falling red blaze leaves up North...

He thinks the suburbs have become purely symbolic
without the characters and plotline and turn of events

Of which he has absolutely no connection
to any belief, feeling, senses, or emotion

A hollow fable where he can literally predict
all the lines and body language of the players....

In effect the suburbs really *is* the antithesis
to the core essence of righteous and true Buddhism
as it has all the affected and artificial forms of emptiness
and nothingness, yet its pathetic and helpless citizens
always seem bent on just playing roles acting all angry
and aggressive, defensive and demonstrative without
soul spending an (in)complete lifetime trying to acquire
possessions and one up their neighbor, a whole different
distorted sort of emptiness and nothingness, hackneyed
half-holy, hollow, and hostile, whose actions (inaction)
and appearance(s) eventually reap the opposite...

He thinks of that hackneyed saying—
"Imitation is the sincerest form of flattery"
but sees nothing sincere about it and who
the fuck really even wants to be flattered?

Crazy is just as far as you are willing to take
the overbearing repetitive sanity
of everything around you...

He thinks where I live on this dead end is like some grand absurd chess game where little bored neighbors align with each other, most spread awful and juvenile parasitic gossip and rumors, and the independent thinker is branded a freak or troublemaker, ridiculously alienated for not being a part of the ritualistic and routinized system (ironically paradoxically with their pure and pathetic lack of communication) but the true-blue delusional thing in living in places like these is no move is ever really made, there's no intellectual or cognitive growth and development, and never leave the proverbial chessboard towards any real sort of other elevated (parallel) plane of being or presence...

It is cruelly ironic and even a little crude and vulgar
and fucked-up and perverse and paradoxical how
it is 'the tourist' who is the one who is actually
abusive and makes the searcher and wanderer
(the loner and constant seeker of knowledge)
continually feel like some sort of criminal or
outsider; don't know, just seems to come to
them naturally from their ignorant and insular
and spoiled and obnoxious worlds to try and
ostracize and make others feel small; couple
words of advice for those who go it alone
never feed into the vicious cycle of abuse
coming from the tourist from hell and this
very upstanding citizen of civilization 101...

Suburbia: now knows why they invented
the roller skate & skateboard, scooter

tension-fatigue syndrome
bird outside window

with arthritis who moans
& groans & cracks his bones

barking dog through screen door
(everybody's getting divorced...)

strange tutor shows up to door
same bat time, same bat channel

to teach you logarithms
and raid your refrigerator

sober girl
stoned

-You wanna do a Bronx run?
-Yeah, why not? Sure...

then go under the pool
like that *Twilight Zone*

where that boy takes
off to never-never land

and never
returns home...

The natural order out here appears 1.drink and 2.cheat on the wife 3.buy them a dog or 4.pool or 5.cruise or 6.have another kid to try and make up for all you did 7.for all you did not do 8.move off dead end 9.get a divorce 10.never be seen or heard from again...

He wonders the rate and percentage of women
who live on the cul-de-sac or dead end
of the homeowner's association
and the frequency in which
and in what contrivances
or mechanisms for purposes
of coital stimulation or arousal
of pleasure during masturbation
i.e. fingers, vibrators, or pieces of
furniture, which have been mandated
or expected to be kept in perfect order
(or those of which this human dynamic
and function does not even cross their
consciousness) against the demographic
of the husband or 'provider' who has pre-
sented as faithful (or gives the impression
of) and has not remained faithful (or
does not give the impression of)...

Thinks the terrible thing about living
(if that's what you'd call it) out here
is that it's all artificial with everyone striving for
superficial perfection (and self-importance) feeling
at the same time you're gradually sliding and regressing
losing your basis for comparison; what gets you in the end...

It is funny feels so much more like an outsider
in here in the suburbs than ever did out there
in the city living amongst a million strangers...

On how to renovate a haunted house: watch out on how they'll try to make you hate and doubt yourself even not belong (to yourself) but got every right to love and respect yourself (when swear all you ever did was mind your own business and struggle and go it alone and never give up and try to contribute something good and positive to this world) so beware got plenty of tricks up your sleeve that they were simply asking for and just never should have thought to ever cross...

Noah's Arks sit on front lawns
actually bigger than the homes
with those satellite dishes all
over them to get reception
perched on top like awful
bird's nests radiating
to the stars like
the cognitive
delayed reality
of its citizens
being stuck
somewhere
between paranoia
& what it means
to think & believe
they know it all
(the absurdity
and distorted
point-of-view
of pointless
suburbia)
more so prefers
seeing it as image
of those drag queens
he finds more interesting
from the meat market
in the city right around
the dimly-lit windows
& old time sawdust
floors of the bagel
shop at dawn
who hustled
& haunted
& really added
& contributed
their literal
spirit & soul
& even humility
& raw sense of humor
to the historical cobblestone
& character of the neighborhood
throwing their hands out to sea

and going "Land, ho"
where the fiddler
and chimneys
used to be...

He thinks if the fiddler were around today he'd climb up
to that rooftop with that fiddle to get away from it all and hit
his dome on some satellite dish and go what the fuck is this?
Shit! Mutter some curse word in Yiddish while going tumbling
down from his slate roof back down to earth where they keep
the pigs and after he shook his head trying to make sense of
it seeing the homes all aglow the worst sort of brainwash the
worst kind of pogrom of its cookie-cutter citizens in the little
nutshell of a shtetl all placated and sedated and would never
feel more at a distance more isolated more alone and more
defeated matter of fact wouldn't even care less about
if I was a rich...

Lives in *locoland* where dealers make their exchanges
in front of the manic crossing guard winding her arms
non-stop back and forth like a windmill coo-coo clock
gone haywire all in front of this perfectly still Japanese
Maple in the drizzle draped in front of some pristine
box-shaped rectangular milky-white aluminum siding
home; the delinquent boys and bright-eyed tomboy
girls going back and forth in their seductive rapport
walking home not sure who started it all and the dead
those mean and miserable middle-aged housewives
who never ever look satisfied or happy to be alive
with no expression and flat affect looking to take hostages
in the tanks their husbands purchased for them so what?
So what happens when everything everyone turns to a possession?

Out here they got these drive-thru confession booths
and always wondered what the passengers in there
were consuming while they were confessing their
sins? A huge falafel? One of those chalupas at
Taco Bell? A bucket of the colonel's best? Big
sloppy Baconater from BK? A fish fillet pulled
straight from the sea? And when they find
out their fate whether they get absolved
or extra homework and gotta repeat their
Hail Marys and wipe the special sauce from
their mouths and then zoom out to cause more
unnecessary drama and harm and ruin more lives...

It turns out the people with the same name who just ended up taking the same place as the people with the exact same name and the head of the association who got impeached due to certain improprieties and whole family excommunicated from the dead end these new people with the same name end up becoming the new head of the association and that guy who used to live here with the same name turns out insanely ended up embezzling the other guy's money cashing in on all his dividend checks and royalties from his liquidated chocolate milk company and now the new guy with the same name is forced to end up moving as one of those people who really believes strongly in karma and just goes to show doesn't much matter how good you are (how much you mind your own business) how absolutely really nothing absurdly literally changes here at all how the shape and configuration of this dead end of human nature of the fucked-up nature of humans becomes like some real-life crude and vulgar psychotic parable of that proverb what goes around comes around...

He views poor relationships with family
like when the fortune cookies started
going with those plastic wrappings...

In America you now have whole towns and brand new uniform
homogenized cities set up and structured and planned to
conform and revolve around The Mall, and in all the tourist
catalogues and relocation packages this will represent the safe
and stable meeting place and cultural Mecca, the postmodern
efficient town square, authentic and air-conditioned, getting
any and all of your needs and desires met, having any possible thematic international fast-food you could possibly wish
for, playing eternal symphonies and muzac (and can meet
your first girlfriend; that blind date who will prove to
be your lifelong companion) and a good place to bring
or even better yet drop off the high-end wife and children...

It (the mall) is a sort of strange and obscure Shangri-la a very pristine and organized Heaven for the Caucasians where one feels nihilistically detached, eternally a part of this sort of repetitious *Myth of Sisyphus*, where you believe the more and more you stroll round and round like a hamster in his wheel the more you might feel a part of culture, that first feeling and smell and senses which hit you after spending a night in jail, representing a very abstract and organized and institutionalized and illusory-like freedom, as we move from store to store, home to home food stand to food stand, girl to girl (who would ever want to leave this beautiful denial and procrastination of the ultimate end?) Old men stare off in the distance sitting at that artificial wishing well patiently waiting for something (for something that will never come or worse off will...) with all the loose change thrown in and forgotten and settled at the bottom before they turn on the oasis-like fountain and would much rather be fishing...

Black pimps pick up white girls...

Speed walker stalks jogger on the promenade
trying to catch up to her in one of
those up and coming areas...

This does not show up in the relocation package...

Thinks the damage the eternal fatigue is starting to catch up with him and be the one at the fried clam stand where the young pretty girls are starting to feel sympathy and sad and bad and flirting with him and with his filthy cherubic beautiful boy and girl with the curly blonde flaxen hair and chocolate all over faces and missing front teeth and wife eternally mad and they load back into the car and they already got it all figured out and planned...

The rabbits the morning after Memorial Day and god blessing
of America and ceremonies at all the graveyards and mausoleums and parades for the o so holy and sacred police
benevolent association and local fire station who love to speed
through red lights during their lunch break and stand like
a bunch of very stern and serious GI Joe soldier crossing
guards in their ten-gallons for what they spoon feed you
are all our heroes finally come out of their holes and take a
breather and a sigh of relief and return them to their grief
with those obsessive lawn mowers and weed whackers and
leaf blowers and packs and engines and long vacuums to get
practically every possible piece of nature off the ground; the
throwing of slabs of beef and dogs and chicken and corn on
the grill while the very competitive parents with their loveless
marriage are policing their o so precious good and virtuous
kids attacking each other from parochial school around the
jungle gym going in for the kill and you never ever quite
see them just a bunch of Charles Schultz nutjob parents
punitively screaming and hollering and threatening through
the screen doors of the kitchen; the cars and appliances
and all those things which make people feel better and more
comfortable and safe and secure are all on sale and everything
must go "to make room for the new" coming through the door
like some revolving pimp land-ho arrival all brought to you
and powered by *The Home Depot*

You wonder if there is any room
for you at all down that hole...

Teenage twin sisters of seduction
flogging each other over the head
with their batons on their lawn
with a stand-up satellite dish
and stand up version of Virgin Mary
in the corner; There is a developing
crowd and story and neighbors and
splattered blood on their cheerleading
uniforms with shock and tears and a bit
of remorse (and a new-found respect)
and possible concussions or comas
and witnesses and ambulances

Those red plastic cups to fill up your beer with
and batons like scattered bones
you'd find at an excavation

Helicopters drowning out motorcyclists
when the switchblade light of dusk
comes to gobble them all up...

Flesh
spread out
like fresh fish
in a pan around
the local community pool
the dynamite stand for the 4th
dressed in red white and blue
assistant fire marshal
telling you what to do...

You got to know kung-fu to survive this life
be one of those dudes hiding out in *Hogan's Heroes*
with the trap door in the floor *The Mod Squad* constantly
on-the-run running through haunted subterranean labyrinths
and sewers like some recurring dream and nightmare Leo
Gorcey the wise cracking wise ass "Over the river and I'll
see you in the funnies!" Injun Jim floating in mid-air
slow-motion backwards through the shattered glass
of the courtroom making a mad dash for it
from the old boy network...

He wonders do all the tree frogs who suddenly come
out with their eloquent symphonies have the need
to be on their mini lawnmowers like humanity

with their earplugs and goggles and motors
strapped to shoulders mowing and mulching
the mote around their lovely little kingdoms?

Man-o-man-o-shewitz when you really
look at it and urge you not to the king is so dumb
king so dumb king so dumb king dumb king dumb.

Spends his time inside the rainbow
watching his back with razor
blade under tongue

Looks forward to the exploding package
but all he gets are those blood oranges
from his aunt down in Boca...

While on the treadmill
on his local cable he sees
from the corner of his eye
"Corned Beef Supper, Those Hurt
By Same Sex Attraction, Curbside Drizzling"
some weather girl a complete knock-out matter
of fact a whole mountain range telling him about
the possibility of pop-up thunderstorms and thinks
even though he doesn't know exactly what those are
loves the sight and sound of them and just once for
a little short while to get caught up with her in pop-
up thunderstorms with Nellie (Spanish last name)
in possible pop-up thunderstorms...

His reality becomes beautiful nymph tomboy girls
with their tight pants on & sneakers & ponytails
& precious & perfect bodies & budding bosoms
& great big brooding grins he views as blushing
murals working the lanes at the *Bowl-o-rama*
for kid's friends birthday parties trying to get
to know a little more about the life & culture
out here chatting away with mothers working
and trying so hard to desperately maintain and
hold on to husbands who just never ever really
seem to literally be there in mind body & spirit...

The very handsome Mexican mountain climber
with his harness still on takes a breath of fresh air
and is reflective under an awning in the rain so far
away from his family and country outside one of these
children's thematic get-the-energy-out birthday parties.

He seems like he's seen it all and these types of things
just appear to trigger how he feels so lost and alone...

To get away and get somewhere else he remembers those days
when he used to engage in certain wild and crazy escapades
of intimacy with a distinctively different variety of women
and the most intriguing and inspiring thing was their vast
mix and multiplicity of beauty, menageries of color and
shape and texture; the size and depth of pussy, blonde,
red, peach, deep succulent sea, how each particular
one smelled and tasted, a warm and wet welcoming
retreat, tasty treat with something that boiled blissfully
beneath, crisp and clean, nasty and filthy; each one had
their own personality, beauty of the beast, beast of beauty,
radiant and ripe, receptive entity, the wonderful and wild
whimsy simplicity of their being which made him always
feel complete, how ecstasy was that exact moment where
mortality suddenly met eternity, how all things screamed
from the sweet snatch of vulnerability and everything seemed
relieved, redeemed from a mixed-up mind which magically
turned to some bright blooming belly, all uncertainty to
possibility, how the finally fulfilled unfulfilled fantasies
freed him from the burden of reality; talk about true
hospitality? One's identity? Having the ability
to believe without really having to be?

He thinks the great thing when he first got laid
and had sex and made love is that it took all those
self-conscious character flaws and imperfections
and made them all seem perfect if that makes
any sense at all to finally realize and discover
that things don't really need to be perfect
or make any sense at all...

The great thing about dreams and fantasies
is that they're a blissful explosion that break

through 'practically' every rule and
regulation that was ever man-made...

The language and dialect we pick up from past girlfriends
the inner and external cadences and rhythms, as if suddenly
being released from acquired societal and familial burdens
and a natural explosion of unknown linguistic freedoms;
what we naturally hear ourselves out of bliss and wonder
relaxation and self-soothing saying without even knowing
matching and coinciding with their shape and personalities
like some inner dialogue which has always somehow been
hidden inside and suddenly comes out much to our surprise...

Every new relationship was like a new life
a new beginning a new romance a new
madness new sadness a new neuroses...

He thinks about that girl from The Lower East Side
who used to runaway all the time this rich girl from
Pennsylvania who ironically ran away to Penn station
and would deliver nice bags of weed on her bike from
Sellasie I from the Rastas on 12th between Avenue C
and Avenue D to all the wealthy Caucasians who decided
for some reason wanted to be hip and move to The East
Village like some sort of instant fix paper route made
her good pocket money and now being and feeling
totally alienated and lost and fucked up out here
in the suburbs in the *Land-O-Lakes* land of nowhere
probably similar to where she lived sometimes dreams
that someone could just come by to rescue me deliver me
maybe a nice chai tea or a bundle of d. maybe even a little
rum for my rum and Coke when I just feel real down in the
dumps and got nothing to look forward to and can come by
while I was watching my weather channel ask if they want a
little of my leftover chicken and *Uncle Ben's* rice do they need
to use the bathroom and then dig right in to my easy chair
and watch the developments coming in from the Midwest

Always makes for the best leftovers
left right on top of my refrigerator...

Wife's a fine girl and has made these nice little sandwich baggies of Cheerios or Lucky Charms for when Dylan has his fix and gets home from school; Reminds him of when he used to cop and pick up nickel and dime bags out in The Bronx; Every man needs to get down on his knees and thank his lucky stars...

He whispers aloud—

"Baby all I've ever tried
is have you live the dream,
the lie, the mirage. If I can't
make you happy I'd rather die. Sigh.
I dreamt I was a very old man last night..."

Moon over shoulder
moon in my mind

Moon never let me down
at my lowest of times...

Sometimes he knew it had absolutely nothing at all
to do with a full moon but probably a lack of moon
a lack of weather a lack of truth just some old timer
wandering out to his yard with headphones glued on

Whizzing chainsaw and cutting down all the branches
from his tree for no particular reason just the mood
that he's in then heads back in for a cup of coffee
a cup of beer no matter both will do the trick

Defrosting roadkill from freezer
and will make some sort
of smorgasbord.

On days like these
he thinks of that stalking ice cream man
strange goings-on in the bookmobile and The Fonze taking
off in mid-air over those garbage cans never coming down.

Often it's got absolutely
nothing to do with
a full moon at all...

Waiting for the fucken moon to howl back!
(There are those who will try to damage you forever
Funny, always seem like the ones who are the least clever...)

He thinks it's kind of funny out here all the people he's
supposed to take seriously could never take too seriously
and even opens the door to mockery and those who appear

kind of fragile and forgotten and the people people like to
forget about finds himself taking more seriously and drives
through the suburbs like Batman in his Batmobile street=
wise watching his back; Inspector Cluseau

with his fare share of paranoia, *Everything runs on Dunkin*
then pleasantly places his blanket in the stray cherry picker
right by a sign which reads "Thickly Settled" below some

grotesque satellite dish which sits fixed on top
some little ranch-style aluminum-siding home
and lives happily ever after inside and outside

there where there's
never ever really
any war or weather

A whole town actually run by the girl's field hockey team
running up and down the sidewalk while the grownups
are getting ready for their token showdown

when the sun goes down
in front of the cameras
on your local cable...

He views everyone out here on this little lollipop of a dead
end bent and obsessed with getting their U.P.S. and Fed-Ex
deliveries on a daily basis almost like some kind of extension
to their empty lives and existences, one day he's gonna just
lose it and have them back it up back down his driveway
and drop the plank and out come the dancing elephants
the giraffes the lions the bears and monkeys with their
accordions maybe even one of those barkers with a top hat
and elastic man and little men and the lady with the beard
and very appropriately a stickie on the garage door saying
Please Leave Here

That'll show 'em...

At times feels like domesticity (even that word bothers me)
suburbs is a prison all the bullshit and stressors
life sentence which ain't never gonna end

Neighbors you wouldn't wish on your worst enemy...

He feels like he always has been and started off so receptive and complete and well-rounded and how they try to turn you ignorant and incomplete and fragmented; How that there is one of the biggest and most subtle of crimes of all time...

To a certain extent views 'domestic violence' as non-stop repetition with the same everyday draining routines and rituals surrounded by people he has nothing in common with and absolutely no respect for and an environment which provides absolutely nothing new or spontaneous (or something to look forward to) ultimately the mani= festation of the denouement to the existential crisis...

He thinks in marriage you argue about some of the most trivial shit and so when it gets down to it is it really an argument or for that matter an issue or perhaps something deeper even more shallow.

He views history as well as not complex or complicated but pretty simplistic and a power-struggle of ideologies and systems and a lack of tolerance; empty glitzy piano lounge with the exact same gossip and rumors and characters and regulars and losers and studs and hangers-on...

Thinks never particularly fond of that expression *having the patience of a saint* as in his opinion in retrospect most saints he knew were pretty damn impulsive with the demeanor of a criminal and those with patience plotting and predictable...

He thinks he has dealt with people with pieces of shit like this
to last a lifetime. He thinks he hates expressions like 'enough
to last a lifetime' as doesn't begin to describe and the biggest
understatement of all time. He thinks he loves the old image
of the young and handsome Mohammed Ali doing the rope-
a-dope leaning back on the ropes giving the impression of
letting his opponent get the better of him really pretending
and being stronger and in much better shape than him
the philosophy of wearing down his opponent letting
him throw all those punches then in later rounds just
jumping off the ropes and out of nowhere with a couple
quick flashes and counters bringing the crowd and
broadcasters and all of America to its feet and knocking
him out topping it off with a hysterical rant of I'm so
pretty I can't possibly be beat very much along the lines
of I've dealt with enough people like this to last a lifetime...

He could never get or ever quite get or just didn't want to get or instantly forget this breed of selfish and greedy (the worst possible combination of traits he could possibly think) why they seemed to expend all this energy in trying to be mean I mean why did they spend all this time in trying to be mean I mean what do they mean and always seemed like they just didn't quite exactly know themselves and proverbially get what they were saying or classically and clinically incomplete and sublimated all that pain and hate they tried to inflict on him from some deep-seated envy and jealousy and insecurity to rise up and be quick-witted and a wise ass and acting-out and at-risk and self-destructive and charming and the one all the parents warned their kids about and wanted them to stay away from ironically was clever and smart enough to even charm them...

He could never understand and remained eternally confused
suppose very similar to how the Native-American ended up
feeling (or not feeling) about this species who seemed to be
obsessed with 'territory' and would do anything humanly
(or not human) possible to make it look all perfect and neat
and tidy and get on hands and knees and instantly whip out
all their very expensive equipment they purchased and treat
like acquired treasures that should be worshiped from their
man shed their lawnmower so that grass looks like some sort
of perfect carpet like some extension to their furniture not
moved an inch out of place whip out whatever else mechanical
they can get their hands on the chainsaw the weed whacker get
every trace and remnant of nature off the ground with the
leaf blower and engine attached to back goggles and hat of the
omniscient groundskeeper and get it looking like some sort of
ball field or stadium or park or museum or institution get it
looking like some perfect painting hanging on the wall (that
they can also control) so as to give the impression that people
might worship them but are so busy trying to 'one-up' and
beat (and be mean to their neighbor) in a very aggressive and
competitive manner ironically don't say a word or get to know
them in getting it to look like some picture perfect postcard
and might even glare and start wars and strangely enough
out of a natural and insular paranoia and phobia and
delusional-like behavior treat them like 'strangers' (and
project all their shit onto them) for maybe even perhaps
staring in their direction when it is not by coincidence
when they are 'in culture' exhibit the exact same behavior
as what they also somehow consider to be an extension to
their territory and bring their attitude and privilege and
entitlement along with them like a herd of cookie-cutter
tourists and will literally look over the people and natives
and aborigines who originally inhabited that land and aloof
and arrogant body language and expressions will indicate how
they 'don't give a damn' about anything or anyone around
them and will pretend to even look through and over these
people who contributed and gave everything to what other
possible 'territories' might they be able to see and steal and
swallow up and claim for themselves for their lovely All-
American spoiled and obnoxious family for their little
safe and secure kingdom because of course it's all and

always only been about them and are such good and caring
providers and family men who just care so much about the
sanctity and security of their family and future and what
they can pass on to them and don't care who they have
to sacrifice and slaughter in this mock medieval system
in order to get it...

He remembers just seeing recently this real keen documentary on *The Fab 5* that brilliant team of freshman from the early nineties from The University of Michigan with Jawan Howard and C. Webb and Jalen Rose and Jalen who said it all (about the people in life who try to make you feel small) how much he couldn't stand Duke because he felt like the institution or coach only gave scholarships and favoritism to Uncle Tom's and how his mother had to slave like 20 hours a day and for some reason the people who for unfair and cultural reasons will always be 'accepted' by society and he was in the category (probably because of appearance and all misconceived preconceived notions) that will be on 'the outside' and will always hate or alienate and was like wow how he was instantly able to relate to this African-American freshman who just said it all...

He thinks I hate those people who say shit like "I have
absolutely no regrets" like I don't trust them and trust them
about as far as I can throw them or a country mile how he
never understood those expressions about as far as I can
throw them a country mile I'd like to throw them a country
mile guess meaning I really don't trust them at all as for
me all my life has been regrets one regret after another after
another after another with a hell of a lot of true-blue remorse
and reflection just trying to make it or maybe more so just
feeling eternally cursed and cheated so yeah I guess it's
not so much about regrets just constantly on the run
from that feeling of feeling eternally cursed and
cheated and done wrong...

If only their sarcasm was a bit more clever
but it isn't and malicious and simply reveals
them as being a part of the mediocre masses...

He thinks out here there is such a queer and bizarre and quixotic psychological phenomena where they try so hard to desperately fit in and belong that they will actually go out of their way to try and make you feel like you don't fit in and belong like this must feel worse than what it feels like to feel like a ghost cause at least with them they can be left the hell alone and do their fair share of haunting and payback and just fucking them up...

He thinks after one of those really long days out here
coming out the shower and shaving his bronzed dome
why do they only show in those beauty salons busts of
those chic and cosmopolitan girls and why not some ruddy
ex-con who just got out of jail and veritably paid his dues?

He misses getting his hair cut at dusk for five bucks
at that hair cutting school on Third Avenue as always
felt real casual and great conversation and made him
feel at home...

He could never really relate or get down
with that clichéd reflective and sentimental
melodramatic portrait of the pouting clown

but thinks what might make this image resound
just a little more sound if you just took off that
makeup and strangely enough found another

pouting clown and took that makeup off
and found another pouting clown
and another pouting clown

A description comes up
over computer which makes
everything more believable...

Dairy Production Specialist
Land O'Lakes
River Falls WI

As some sort of necessary and futile
and desperate escape he thinks back
to his internship as a social worker
at *The Kingsbridge Rehabilitation
Center* in The Bronx somewhere
around the reservoir and this old
man just getting hosed down
somewhere down the hall
and all he heard was
"Wheee!" and that
just seemed
to say
it all...

He remembers during internship people having breakdowns
and meltdowns right there in the chart room where they keep
the diagnoses of those of gloom and doom and literally had
to scoop up fellow students in the fetal position who went
to Yeshiva (casually claiming they were Axis 2) like taking
fish out of the ocean

To him they seemed like the most
interesting and sympathetic...

He could never ever really stand that expression
or never really cared much for *Don't cry over
spilt milk* and thought why not? Why not think
of his old drama queen girlfriend who he once
loved who he once loved to fuck all day
and all night long in her flat in Sleepy
Hollow which sat smack-dab like a
lily pad floating down some foggy
alley with a lovely shabby window
feathered flush up against the booming
lungs of a foghorn which literally and
psychologically allowed him to forget
it all, all the guilt and bullshit that go
brought on by the goddamn good and
gone damage of some dysfunctional
family worst sort of hangers-on...

He thinks back to when he used to casually joke to the night clerk whose wife walked out on him for another woman and became all law-abiding and literal trying to figure out some issue and conflict for an impossible guest on their graveyard shift thinking they got it all figured out just naturally imitating the late-great Inspector Cluseau "The problem is solv-ved" and he angrily snaps back and retorts "The problem is not solv-ved!" this scenario becoming the classic metaphor for his life after taking a Summer job between semesters at *The Wurzweiler School of Social Work* after his mad Borderline girlfriend walked out on him for no particular reason, while the next semester he fell in love with someone much prettier and better (and ended up marrying her) then started falling for him again...

He thinks he's starting to develop
some of the same personality as his fish
who likes to cat-nap and get some shut eye in the morning.

At dusk at the bewitching hour likes to come out and come
alive and when he wants to be left the hell alone
hides away in the rear staircase of his castle.

People always stereotypically talk about
the very sad tragedy of Alzheimer's and Dementia
well I tell you I swear really look forward to losing my mind…

Somehow thinks in the back of his mind
how he always respected and admired
all those who decided (or maybe
not so much a decision as more
so an action) to take their life
as just felt and seemed right
and was totally able to sympathize
with why and wondered why and why
never ever those who really deserved to die?

Thinks...

I always hated when people told me they were praying for me like always made me a little squeamish and stop to think like why were you praying for me and who are *you* to pray for me (I know, I know...) as never found the need and start to think not necessary or taking things way too seriously and don't know what's wrong with me but could never take too sincerely like you were praying for me like using me to do your good deed like some strange form of flattery which makes me feel more distant and lonely...

He thinks he hates those phonies who hit him with such clichés like *don't shoot the messenger* like wasn't even thinking—but seems not by coincidence that they bring up such things and now that you bring it up...

Why doubt is always put in there by the devils
and never the angels but perhaps he's got that
backwards and maybe in fact it is not doubt
at all and something far deeper and shallow...

The one phenomena learned when having lived long enough deep in the heart (of the heartless) of soulless suburbia is that if ever once perhaps in your past maybe as a kid or adolescent you came across or experienced someone who was just a total asshole for no particular reason at all (who appeared to thrive by demeaning and belittling and trying to make other people feel small and being too young to have the intellectual or cerebral *where-with-all* that this is how they really feel about themselves or insecure and often end up taking it out on yourself) you now literally can have a husband and wife team who are a bunch of assholes which seems like an obvious or even for that matter negative statement but really accurate and appear to share and pass on this loathsome, parasitic character and behavior, or trait and characteristic of ignorance and arrogance until it's like they're playing sarcastic snake-in-the-grass tag team literally feeding off each other (and will even lie to each other or not tell each other or give each other information both not by coincidence awful at communication usually incited or provoked by one of these lying assholes keeping it all phony and fragmented) to keep the narrow-minded myth and emotional and spiritual brainwash and form of abuse and attempt at maliciousness and alienation afloat...

From an absurd futile point of view
thinks it's crude how we get judged
by how we acclimate to the mediocre
and the roles we play in the work place
how the mediocre will always rise to power
how we present and function in the public arena
the food market, the chain stores of the strip mall
at the park with those dull-eyed and very loud passive-
aggressive mothers; your social skills at the health club
which seems like just one big sleazy awkward pick-up
of overcompensating young adults pumping up and all
returning home alone; beware if you don't play those
uptight roles of the upstanding citizen or innocent
bystander they'll instantly label you as a freak
or outsider with no room for redemption.

Sometimes he likes to shadow a security guard around
the store for reverse harassment and to teach him
a lesson and to keep him on his guard as he's
always so slow in picking this up not knowing
you're on to him in thinking he's on to you
not knowing what he's getting himself into

You turn his suspicion into confusion...

Who was it Cool J. said?
"Don't call it a comeback
I been here for years!"

Hank Williams?
Kurt Cobaine?
Buddha

Without
hope
or fear

"She war
blue—
Moses!"

Rimbaud coming in
in the slave boat
sneaking a peek
through a port
hole of roses...

Blues is having no blues at all
no real challenges to face at all
by the know-it-alls who have seen
nothing at all what Jean-Paul Sartre
attributed to the eternal 'existential'
emptiness of the world which puts
you at a nihilistic loss Sigmund
at the end of his career who said
he still does not understand a thing
about the female Moses on-the-run
Dostoevsky still planning the perfect
hit and run why men cheat and have
run-ins with the law with The Lord
that big empty hollow knothole
where the wind blows and
you've heard it all before...

He thinks...

Whenever I'm feeling really blue
or down in the dumps or depressed
or think I lost it I think of John Coltrane's
beautiful downtrodden eyelashes like some
tender graceful horse brooding and reflective
man it must have been kinda cool or relieved
a little of the stress of this fucken existence
being a dope addict; I gotta get back on
the right track. I'm convinced my wife
is having an affair with a younger man
or older boy however you want to put it
think how she'd prefer it with her arrested
stage of development (I saw how she
was staring from the corner of her eye
today at the college boys at *Sonic* but who
am I to complain considering the amount...)
and hell what'ya gonna do? She sure as heck
deserves it and is picking us up a submarine
sandwich. Screams down the steps "Be safe!"

Could never really stand that expression *self-esteem* as always seemed to not say a thing and patronizing and made-up and made by those phony motherfuckers who never saw a thing and probably the exact ones who tried to take it in the first place now *fear of intimacy* that's one for the ages...

Wants to be considered the greatest American *fellosopher*
from a life of constant falling and his methodology and
point of view and the way he views the world will be
from this physical and psychological vantage point
how we get on and continue from all that damage
we can't ever get rid of nor really try which continues
to permeate and rape the hardwired consciousness
and those necessary defense-mechanisms and
coping and surviving skills we must take on
kind of the motto of the numb and reactive traits
and characteristics of the inherent rebel shot with bullet
holes through his soul forced to go it alone and the rest
of his life devoted to self-reflection (and observation)
and redemption to try and casually and naturally
fill in those holes one by one by one by one...

He loves how in front of the DSM-IV
the statistic manual for mental health
professionals to pretty much diagnose
mood and personality disorders the editor
actually dedicates it to some chick or girl
some lover or another and always thought
so damn cool and whimsical and unexpected
and wondered about this like never thought
that some actual guy actually wrote or compiled
it something like the dudes who wrote the bible
dedicating it to all the wise men and the fools...

Maytag repairman develops a social phobia...

He gets nauseas when he thinks of 'the model citizen…'

Humanists get on his nerves...

He tries to kiss his wife on the neck
"Stop, I get dizzy on the stairs…"

Not sure why literally the little things in life
which get you somewhere down the line
like bedbugs which get you in the end...

"Mother should I run for president?"
and the burn-outs stumble out
of The Hayden Planetarium...

Wants to see the very poised and perfect and pretty weather
woman just with a very flat and wooden expression saying—
"Expect to see more rain and more rain and more rain and
more rain…" then very casually neatly blowing out her
brains the t.v. screen going blank for a little while
and a commercial for *The Best Western*…

How he's fond of that expression *root of all evil*
as thinks that has a lot to do with our nightmares
and all that shit we have no control over (from
the petty motherfuckers and family dynamics
of dysfunction and alienation and scapegoating
and stigmatization mostly from a Machiavellian
Dostoevskian and Shakesperian point of view)
from all those things which prove to be cruel
and we subconsciously always somehow
somewhere deep down inside knew...

The daughters are pretty All-American girls
who are starting to do those power-strolls
develop very strong opinions of themselves...

Their mothers' cougars seething along the strip mall...

How he always found himself confused by those idiots
waving from their float and the idiots waving back
at them all euphoric and such; To just think
of that simple image when breaking it down
a float rolling through the center of town
with a bunch of happy idiots and a stream
of hysterical idiots lining the streets waving
back at them all proud and safe and sound...

He thinks living out here
in the suburbs everything feels like
some long drawn-out form of domestic abuse...

The crow outside window
only one he can connect to
so deep and black and blue
minding his own business
pecking at the earth all day
long before and after the storm
and then moving on, some call 'em
moon pies some call 'em scooter pies...

His long sigh with bloodshot eyes
is the clock tower in a town
with no people alive...

Thinks if those who kill themselves do so because they think the world would be a better place without them what would a rebirth look like?

Life like a bad dream with a fox
on your lawn before the storm...

The wind a leftover piece of rug galah...

Prayer a hypothetical question...

He and his wife lighting the candles before the hurricane
and gets to thinking don't really give a damn about the
humans really don't as never really been too human from
my experience but what happens to all the wild animals
during hurricanes then suddenly out of nowhere sees this
great big snowy figure just squatting there in the distance
in silhouette some beautifully snowy-blue coyote like a
stark vision through the slider doors of his kitchen just
kind of casually cocking his head back and forth looking
all ominous yet also luminous just hanging there in the
middle of the wild and whipping winds his great big torso
of fuzzy sky-blue fur and glowing eyes on the edge of the
forest just minding his own business looking down into
the perfectly manicured backyards with all their little token
spoiled brat jungle gym equipment and those mean and fierce
yet self-soothing god-like winds blowing all around up there
in the treetops and feels there is nothing more that he can
possibly connect or relate to in the moment or for that
matter in retrospect in this artificial fucked-up environment
(ironically more bent on brutality and cruelty and destruction)
than this beautiful solitary creature just standing there like
some guardian or beacon representative of everything real
and righteous and instinctive on the border of the radiant
wilderness and awful nauseating suburb which spiritually
kills people on a daily basis...

Thinks would have loved
the fiddler on the roof
singing the ballad
to West Side Story
that one—*Who
knows? Could be...*

Pissing out back door of the basement during the hurricane
the only time only thing that ever makes any sense to him
work shoes like he's been wrestling with alligators
could curl up in the pews of the train station
best memories are the bums
nuns of his consciousness...

Wants to hide behind the menagerie
behind the shadows and scene
ready or not here I come
how many licks
did it take to get
to the center?

Remembers that strange brutal recess all the way back to grade school to the hot-top asphalt when those girls in like the third or fourth grade literally stripped down for them each article of clothing one by one by one until buck-naked behind the hedges along the brick wall of the school and somehow strangely feeling taken advantage of, manipulated and controlled and still even a little confused to what brought it on watching all the boys literally jumping up and down pushing each other and practically foaming at the mouth...

The rumor just a little later on of that boy getting a blowjob by the waterfall from that girl and trying to and not able to picture or imagine and what kind of blowing was involved?

Like some surreal paint-by-number
he had always loved and which had
suddenly out of nowhere got ripped off...

The babysitters who taught him how to smoke cigarettes
and when he started to choke on it
tried to wash it down with milk...

Remembers disco being like this young teenager
and hearing songs like *good times these are the
good times* and not feeling at all like good times
but feeling more like really depressed and down
in the dump times and being so out of touch with
his feelings feeling even more melancholy when
Donna Somers used to come in at the end of
ceremonies and bellow her swan song symphony
Last Dance at the close of bar-mitzvahs feeling like
he should have gotten someone and was really a
good catch and good looking kid and having so
much to offer and having felt like his whole life
had passed him by and passed right in front of his
eyes and got absolutely nobody and actually even
feeling a bit angry and guilty that he had let down
some idealized expectation of him which was
around the age of 13 whereas in the Jewish
tradition a boy becomes a man and feeling
like all these idiot kids were getting them
and knowing for sure these were not the
right men and maybe even knowing subconsciously deep down inside was like
some sort of archetypal microcosm or
premonition of what soon was to come...

He always wondered about all this and would he have to get this and how was he going to get it and is this what it meant by happiness and felt repulsed and petrified by it and by the nature and violence of it and by its natural opposites nihilistically became the eternal romantic...

Looking back as a kid having sex at a very young age almost found a bit intimidating but of course being a guy didn't want to admit it as almost seemed more like some aerobic exercise or competition as opposed to having something to do with compassion and true love and sympathetic by very aggressive white girls determined and driven...

Thinks it's funny how
he always focused
so much better
in summer school
think it had something
to do with the weather
or the people who weren't
there and swear aced it all
and even ended up loving
math & science & social
studies like some ragged
beat-up explorer beat up
from the high seas after
the whole lowly crew
was dead & gone after
some mass mutiny
man if you saw
those perfect
parabolas
I drew
and all
those proofs
I ended up proving
Teddy Roosevelt
throwing his hat
in the ring
rolling bones
somewhere
around
the Lou-
weese-
anna-
terror-
tree
head
of the
Miss-
iss-
ippi
foot of
Rockies
Bewt

Montana
Boise
Black hills
North by
northwest
Dakota
some
where
around
The Platte
& Red River
difference
between
the bison
& buffalo
stampede of
sunbathers
in Florida
Mafia in
Chicago
who assured
Kennedy's
election
& the bullets
that always
made us
remember
think I even
thought a little
bit about my future...

He thinks back all the way to High School and French class and those girls with their seductive acts at the end of class with their pretend stretches pushing their chest all the way up to the ceiling while showing the boys everything their shapes and contours and beauty and what they chose to (not so) secretly be doing and be revealing. Some of them were cheerleaders who didn't like each other and he now pretended to see them together without their sweaters entwined naked flat-chested and voluptuous. He preferred the one flat-chested as she was kinder and nicer and would actually sit on top of his lap in the back of class while he would get all aroused and erect and could still feel that boner could still feel his boner on her was boning her and she would just sit there while the professor was conjugating irregular verbs and pretended like nothing was happening but both knew exactly what was happening which made it all that much more exciting. He wondered where she was now. Wondered where he was now...

Thinking back to being a teenager developing certain odd work habits having the addictive habit some might call it a hobby of sorts of stealing from stores and malls and had to change the store policy at *J.C. Penny's* for him him being pretty proud of that he and his friends going in trying on layers and layers of Izod Lacoste and Polo shirts and with a smile pleasantly strolling off to pick up the local bus back looking back not even really knowing what he was doing actually making him feel closer to home and more down to earth with society natural reaction (what the mandated psychiatrist referred to as "acting-out" and "at-risk behavior") of a very controlling and domineering father my naive angelic mother asking when she opened up my drawers where did you get all these from don't remember buying them mother's natural proclivity towards denial and gullibility wanting to believe ironically leaving The Who's *Hooligans* on the back seat of the bus...

As a kid gave into sarcasm not really thinking about it
as an instant relief and panacea to heal all that damage
and even abuse of power coming from know-it-all authority
figures who he knew somehow deep down inside however
hard he tried would never nor even care to have the ability
to listen and thus becomes his swan song his solution
cutting them to the quick again not even realizing it
surreal and slick...

How he went through so many relationships
to help him to identify as opposed to define
how looking back there was such a fine line...

He thinks the best thing about being married
the first one who ever really stuck up for me
against all the really stuck-up members of the
family; now what could they really say about me?

Almost as if getting your identity back when it never should have been taken in the first place...

Don't pay particular close attention to pictures in picture frames especially if those people or particular members of the family have a history of bringing the shame and being deceitful manipulative and trivial and petty even power-hungry thus will posture themselves in that particular moment for how they want others to view and perceive them in the future or for some other future moment or memory all a part of that strange and not so sincere picture in the picture frame...

He'd rather think back to growing up on that plush dead end in the suburbs which felt like some eternal summer and those front screen doors that were always kept open like a sort of movie screen in the shadows for kids to run in and out of...

The popsicle stick fence looking as if built by Lincoln logs and the weeping willow which grew up over it and just kept on getting larger and larger as if growing into the heavens separating neighbors backyards making all of childhood just seem that much more glorious and mysterious...

A series of coincidences before ever
having the need to know such definitions...

It all had to do with the detailed hiss and buzz
from way down below from everything above
from the outside world from everything beautiful
and blessed and blissful that a child without even
knowing it would pleasantly take for granted and
remain forever etched in transcendent imagination...

Superhero grounded on ground in uniform
looking and listening to the sound of gliders
in the great blue suburban sky then gradually
vanishing and taking off to the great unknown...

Later on cheeseburgers on back porch
the sound of neighbor's dogs trailing off...

Bug juice
(Hi-C? Kool-Aid?)
What it used to be called...

Then running around in fresh warm clean soft cotton pajamas just out the dryer to get out the last of drama and beginning of dew on the tips of summer lawns before entering slumber...

He could still smell the mud and marigolds...

The miracle of the folds of the flower in foyer window...

Folded back, inwards, which would protect him
when he felt at his most desperate and vulnerable...

The gunpowder from party snappers
he used to throw at the math teachers
when backs were turned to blackboard...

The difference of true/false...

The falsehood and true lack of free choice in multiple choice...

The real life experience of addition by subtraction...

Addiction for distractions...

Irrational numbers...

Where separation-anxiety started and ironically ended...

He thinks everyone to him seems like a big freaken remainder what happened to those word problems which were supposed to provide a real sense of truth and clarity and lucid thought pattern and logic and linear system of thinking for the future and actually thinks back to his childhood how they all seemed pretty damned futile and just a big waste of time and always frustrated and didn't give a fuck about Midge and her widgets and eventually ironically didn't care about the factors which led up to it the overall equation whether he came up with a solution or not and maybe that's just it...

It eventually amazes him how corrupt and fucked-up people really are so why even try to figure them out?

He would revisit this or maybe just didn't at a future
(imperfect) date at bar-mitzvahs returning home all
stunned and bewildered from roller discos just
trying to keep up with the opposite gender...

Childhood was all your dreams dancing with your nightmares on the edge of blissful despair; all those old holy slapstick comedians come to life in those original silent films

Somewhere around The Lower East Side where they still haven't completed that bridge on drunken midnight East River and considering jumping it to get home to Brooklyn...

Wonders why those who try
to make you feel like a criminal
always in real life *are* the biggest criminals?

Usually little cocky men of grandiose visions...

He thinks is there any possible way to kill himself
with a slingshot believes would be so damn nostalgic
and people (even the coroners and neighbors) would
ask questions and a perfect ridiculous way to go

Used to shoot those rubber bands the orthodontists
put in his mouth at the girls he loved in French class...

The only thing he really finds out
when taking his kid around
to the different playgrounds
to get his energy out
is how fucked-up
and damaged
the parents
really are...

He looks out his screened-in screen door over the porch
to the storm clouds above and thinks how much he just
wants to break down and cry aloud suddenly becoming
a trigger to being something like a 6-year old and storming
through the linoleum of the kitchen his hippie mother on
the phone and him in his Superman uniform hollering
Superman! and while running and trying to open up
the glass door at the same time suddenly realizing
really not it was closed and going crashing right
through the window and along with the pieces
of shattered glass having to be picked up and
scooped up and brought to the hospital for
stitches innocent clueless having no idea how
much this would be ominously prophetic for the future...

How existence seems the difference
between ominous and omniscient...

How his teacher tutor probation
officers all used to tell him--"You
could give a headache to an aspirin"

How he smiled and kept it all in
then mocked and made fun of them
of which they told him he'd never amount to a thing

From a Buddhist and mathematical
point of view thanked them for their concern
and told them couldn't agree more with their reasoning...

Tulip trees growing in the middle of cul-de-sac in early spring
Hangs in window naked dying in the early morning
for all the world to see...

A wonderful way to wait for the rain...

Gertrude anytime there's anytime there's anytime
there's anytime *my love life is boring me...*
(Donna Sommers/Barbra Streisand)

It's raining it's pouring...
wash it out with bubblegum
and send it to the navy
or something or somebody
always got the two mixed-up but
looking back does any of that really
looking back he remembers sledding
down that long snowy hill to the back
of the back of those white summer
buildings in the winter which
housed a *Gristede's* pizza
and bagel place he spent
his after school days
hanging out wasting
childhood worrying
about the future
it's raining
it's pouring
wash it out
with bubblegum
and send it
to the navy...

He claims...

I was born in one of those plastic eggs
you get out of one of those machines
in the supermarket I think some time
in the early seventies then stuffed
in a blue jean pocket and put up
on the white slave trade market
don't think they offer those
jobs anymore in lighthouses
and gotta be a member of
the union and think same
goes as well if you want to
be a gravedigger or just simply
join up with the merchant marines
pretty sure my wife's gonna stab me
when she's in one of her moods and
instead of seeing my whole life pass
right in front of my eyes or any that
silly melodramatic crap will just see
that plastic egg go sliding through
and come around full circle and suddenly
realize why I turned to a life of shoplifting...

Parents were those diagram drawings of instructors
showing you the proper way to stretch and lift barbells
in a safe manner and their parents were the c.p.r. dummy
and infamous Heimlich Maneuver known for his maneuvers
escaping the bizarre Czar from the land of no. 2 pencils and
that cross on the cathedral from one of those eternal sky-blue
health manuals and gave birth to me in the form of one of
those glossy elementary school text books in the land of truth
and liberty where I'd declare dramatically the first day this is
gonna be my year to turn it around and never once cracking
one open found cracking one-liners and acting-out and
charming all the hard-up adjustment counselors.

Couple of decades later when returned victoriously
to my old stomping grounds like Eisenhower after
D-Day waving with that ear to ear smile in all
the confetti in that valley of heroes I brought
my pointer and slide projector having way
surpassed the idiot baseline of them
claiming I'd never reach my potential...

He thinks when I go on interviews
why not go packed with a pistol
couple pieces of *Bazooka Joe*
sick of imagining them naked
matter of fact never imagine
them naked; sometimes I like
to imagine myself naked but
never seem to get the job
(thinking of becoming
a Benadryl addict)
wonder how hitmen
are doing in this economy?

Drooo-wzy!

Gets why Burroughs played with pistols
as just made him feel more comfortable
with all those squares and shitheads he
grew up with with all that psychotropic
medication of heroine and medicine
cabinet opium he always had hanging
around for when he felt at his most
desperate and eventual swing of
swinging moods it put him in
but sure did live the life
and got the most out of

While astronauts were blasting off to space
and presidents getting rubbed out assassinated
face down with their face down to the ground
or looking helplessly up to the stars down
on earth down in these here United States
both just as easy to predict both patterns
just as blatant and obvious all starting off
so promising and all ending so damn tragic

Just getting so sick of a lying and dying
grownup world which never ever seemed
to pay off in the long run which all it ever
seemed to be about was lies and betrayal
and control and possession or whatever
that fucken cliché ratio was which dealt with
the equation having something to do with possession

The advertising men & publishing men
with their jet-black hair & blocked hats
& Coke bottle bifocals stuck in peepholes
like Winnie the Pooh burrowing for honey
during heartbreak *Harcourt Brace* lunchbreak

Leftover hangovers & hallucinations & hashish
in a frisbee perfect to go under one of those
Snow-White mock Christmas trees they used to
brandish back in the fifties to make everything
seem just so perfect and pleasing and pristine

Everything reeking from those glistening green
bottles of *Aqua-Velva* & fantasy & wet dreams
& cigarette-stained charcoal-gray undercover
detective suits he used to sport so seriously
growing up in a very prim and proper uptight
white-collar crime low life upper-middle class
Catholic well-to-do workaholic family he couldn't
stand and could never ever really relate or connect
to the exact selfsame reasons he had to turn to
the religion of self-medication with the desperate
need of the needy needle like Christ on a crucifix

Panoramic view
of the traintrack
of Tulsa & Nebraska
& shores of escapist
Tunisia & Casablanca

Where did I leave my sneakers?
Smokestacks swirling
and calling me
to the river

Best times to go fishing with the madmen at midnight
literally at the end of Manhattan when just had to get
out of my sweltering apartment with a 40 in a brown
paper bag going down like *Manishewitz* and view of that
extended relative from Brooklyn beautiful blaring Statue
of Liberty which has always permeated and stayed with
me from youth to a life of crime to the present to the end
of time growing up a N.Y. boy and that tired drained sun
coming up (going down) over The Hudson & cobblestone
of Pitt St. & Hester peddling my bike blissfully hysterically
down the empty breezy fading streetlight street with my
catch just to catch a snatch of early morning shut eye

(The boys with black eyes
returning home with their
pool cues from Hell's Kitchen)

Might even be little leftover gizzard
and Chinese fries in the refrigerator

Burroughs walks in and hangs his head
on the hat hook trying to make sense of it
really not giving a Rip Van Winkle about
any of it and just shakes off all the fucken
brainwash devil dust of distorted existence
or better yet their distorted thought patterns
and *littleness* of what they project onto him...

Wonders if Walter Cronkite
ever cheated on his wife?
(Paul Newman did once
and learned his lesson)
They said Barbra Walters
was wild and used to get
down with Henry Kissinger
man imagine what that
must have looked like?
If I was President and
had one of those fireside
chats would have been
the first one to roast
smores or maybe
pull a Miles
with my back
to the camera.
Really wiped out
and glad my wife's
back from visiting
her mom in The Bronx...

After Bernard Baruch
made his first million
his pops was pretty
proud of him
and asked him
what he planned
on doing with it
F.D.R. pretty much
got funded all through his
stay at The White House
by his mother and
Burrough's got
a nice monthly
allowance
from his
old man
to help
support his
heroine habit...

When *Midnight Cowboy*
came out in '69 it got
an X-rating and Dylan
had the original sound
track with "Lay Lady Lay"
got into some sort of
contract dispute and
gave it to that dude
who crooned--"I'm
going where the sun
is shining through
the pouring rain"
when Joe Buck
played by Jon
Voigt who
eventually
won The
Academy
Award
wandered
from the dusty
plains of Oklahoma
to the puffing cigarette
billboards which shot out
plumes of smoke looking out
high up over the madness and
hustle of the flux of Times Square
and was really able to relate to it all...

Old middle-aged whore
who he had sex with
and picked up right
off the sidewalk
outside her apartment
in her ritzy high-rise
in The Upper East Side
and showed them having
sex together and while they
were bumping & grinding
& she was in climax
with her t.v. clicker
under her big flabby
tuckis naturally and
magically switching
channels in the madness
of it all in the late-sixties
from commercials to war
to talk shows of an overly-
manicured exploited toy
poodle getting groomed
and its teeth brushed
for just that little short
while for that five minutes
or so won the academy award
for the best supporting actress...

He wonders what would be the opposite
of charmed I'm sure? Charmed I ain't?
Charmed I isn't? I'd prefer not to?
Yeah I prefer it charmed I isn't
Ratso Rizzo mentoring Joe Buck
on the ways of the world all pain
and suffering on the hustle on the
con game in how to naturally and
casually rip off the status-quo when
they're not looking the hors-d'ouevres
without them even noticing *Load up on the
bologna! Hey how you doing*? Charmed I isn't
never quite making it down to his dream to his
fantasy to The Promised Land of Miami, Florida...

That part at the start
of *Apocalypse Now*
where Martin Sheen
is going mad under
the sweltering ceiling
fan in Vietnam think
whiskey or bourbon
played a role as well
and then after that
half-crazed dizzying
disoriented dance
they come back
to get him for
a whole brand
new do or die
mission like
he's just
the man...

Think when we were born
we were all found dead
or alive in the bath...

O no!
they knocked
down the long
long standing
burnt-down
rollercoaster
and putting
up horrible
condos and
hopefully
they'll
burn down
the condos
soon and put
the rollercoaster
back up again
goddamn
it's like
they
didn't
even ask
the phantoms...

Parteck safeme
mysole under
a streetlamp
just hanging
these daze
swear to god
have felt crucified
no self-pity no lie
like one of those
connect the dots
which show you
exactly where you
got your start and
how you ended up
looking back at your life
all the way to your past
never started one god
damn thing ain't exact
jah rating so maybe they
just sensed I was strong
with the ability to get on
with the ability to get along
grab the bull by the bullhorn?
Used to love that song *Rubber
Band Man* by that band forgot...

Got a slice of The American Dream
but why after experiencing it
constantly feel phenomena
of nausea, puking, dying?
On the stairclimber
at the healthclub
they tell you a funeral
can cost anywhere
in the range of
$9,000 and
the government
will only pay like
$250 of that.
Even after death
they stick you
they get you
with dagger
& stagger
off cloud 9
off the stairclimber
to the parking lot
where a bunch of
wannabe wiggers
of pre-manufactured
anger pretend to be
all intimidating & stuff
& just blow them off
& spit in their general
direction welcoming
an open invitation
just trying to provide
more of a waste of time
like a bunch of semi-retired
bullies from the schoolyard
with nothing else better
to do with their lives.
He decides to take
the scenic route
home to avoid
the stripmall
& head down
the highway

where an idiot cop
slob All-American
Nazi Schmuck
in his ten-gallon
& leather boots
& sunglasses
holed-up
in his speed
trap has caught
another poor soul
probably costing
somewhere in the
ballpark range of...

Sun sometimes
falls like eggs
overeasy
over lives
very difficult
lost and lonely
in towns
in The West
like Reno, Boise
Salt Lake City, Utah
Los Angeles, California
already 82, 83, 84
& it is only 8:13
in the morning
& blinking lights
all drained & faded
erased outside casinos
commuters haven't even
come out for their breakfast
burritos & the bums & winos
still fast asleep on *The Burlington Northern*
thinking of every girl like some ghost who let
them down left them for dead 'dead in their tracks'

Moses still making his way across...

Stick that in your Funk & Wagnell's
remember when Woolworth's
shut down & really felt
down & out used to
wander it for days
in the rain &
would really
ground me
& felt
a sense
of belonging
overlooking
Union Square
on 14th street
in New York City
when Wannamaker's
was one of the biggest
department stores or
something or some
punchline like that...

He thinks
my life
these days
homemade
iced coffee
Chock Full
O-Nuts
City Blend
& chicken bones
wish I had couple
of those Wonder
Woman truth
bracelets
to deflect
all my
triggers...

A pail of crushed angels...
The above-ground pool at the end of the rainbow
The jigsaw puzzle in the frame you have fallen in love with
The railroad station where you pick up your dope to cope
The butterflies come to life from your packet
of wildflower seeds from The Home Depot
Not sure whether to shoot down the helicopters
or if its obsessive devil next door on weed whacker
The statistic and demographic of those who
met and fell in love at the methadone clinic,
anger management, and the dog walking club
Heaven will be very thin slice of bubblegum
they used to put in your baseball cards
just enough not to blow bubbles
but also keep your dream alive
Tap shoes left outside the pagoda
Soaking brassieres on clothesline
of the tiny thinly-sliced ballerina
How to shadowbox in 7 easy
The art of fly-swatting
The art of finding yourself
The art of finding dead bodies
Making great strides
in leaps and bounds
in the field of weather...

He wonders
if Mona Lisa
had ever tried
to take her life
with a couple
slices of
razorblades
the ones she
used to chop
the garlic
and basil
and hysterical
weeping and
wailing being
drowned out
by all things
having to do
with the ghetto
with the fish market
with The Mediterranean
with the gossip and rumors
of widows and hustlers
bewildered
befuddled
huddled over
nude and naked
with pussy dripping
from heat and humidity
from the beating sea
beads forming like
teardrops tumbling
nipples percolating
her flesh and folds
exposed vulnerable
fragile and fragrant
like a rose turned inside
out and then back again
feeling like she hasn't
been touched by
a man in ages
the stages

of wasting away
wailing away
in stand up
clawfoot tub
overlooking
looking over
the brilliant
large and looming
muscular mountains
hugging the heavens
lonely and lonesome
overwhelmed alienated
outside the cracked
cracked open
scorching
shutters
of Palermo
her ear pressed
against the keyhole
of the palm trees
of the avenue
like the echoes
of a conch shell stray
sounds of street urchins
sounding just out of reach
and strangely familiar yet
somehow so distant which
feeds into her conflict of
wanting to be worshiped
left alone anonymous
excruciatingly hollow
clearly knowing
with her solitary
portrait and profile
and posture really
aint got nowhere to go
drunken and buzzed
one of those bad ones
playing impossible role
the decadent daughter
modest and humble
stuck in Cinderella's

splintered slipper
Tom Thumb's thimble
in some luminous
land of lost souls
land of no return
somewhere between
Heaven and Hell
dusk and dawn
looking to
be forgotten
remembered
for sure...

He thinks...

Please put me in jail again
please police harass me
& I'll keep them charmed
& laughing & in the solemn
silence silence them feeling
guilt & remorse for what
they did when all I was
casually asking without
an ounce of fear was
what I had done wrong
only time able to get downtime
little laughter & self-reflection
literally singing Jim Morrison
& quoting Haft-Torah
& Buddhist Chants
& Puerto Rican friends
when the drag queens
were escorted in
& strutted in
all demonstrative
& effeminate in shotgun
Spanish Spanish translation
blasting *woman without tits*!
them getting getting them
all worked up & dramatic
actually felt kind of bad for
them dreaming of the first
meal you were gonna get
when they were gonna let
you out imbibing taking in
the fresh clean air hosed
down sidewalks on Hester
beneath sunlit tenements
not sure what day it was
what morning which made
it all that much more pleasant
falling asleep drifting off to the
rhythm of the crashing Coney Island
waves tumbling through your window

first good night good day's rest you got
in awhile with mattress on the linoleum...

Those soldiers
were brave
who piled
into that
great big
wooden
Horse of Troy
Raid on Entebbe
rain on earlobe
stuffing bundle
of heroine into
stuffed animal
to make a living
me me thinks I'm
gonna just creep
into the belly
of Radioflyer
racehorse
to try and make
a name for myself
they don't make
love & war
like they
used to
anymore...

Swears in domestic life
greatest time is right
before I climb up on
the treadmill at night
and piss out the crack
of the cracked open
back playroom door
and shake it all off
soaring up above
the moonlit tree
house across
starry universe
and take in all
the little kid
old man
pungent
smoky
wilderness
like those times
I used to get drunk
all by my lonesome
and wander all through
the broken land of Brooklyn
just him and the foghorns
and in his solitary
musings felt
like he knew
it all and in that
moment he *did*
know it all
discovering
that true blue
wisdom is knowing
that there's really
soaring up above
nothing to know
at all and this
moment just
pissing out
the back
door after all
the mishegoss

thrown into
the forgotten
blessed silence
with the sudden
image of those
tranquil rolling
clouds and smoky
forest and tree frogs
actually means more
than 'anything at all'
all at a blissful loss...

Piano tutor charges by the minute
That's pretty precise isn't it?
Like Beethoven being
in harmony with nature
Mozart with the heavens
and Tchaikovsky with the seasons
He misses his internship when he
used to flirt with all the young cute
girls from Yeshiva who he knew
he'd never be able to get with
and for that reason they used to
flirt with him even more almost
as if he was forbidden and
he kind of liked it almost
made it less obvious and
more romantic misses
working at that clinic
in The Bronx with
the Schizophrenics
at lunch eating Dominican
and dreaming of his future…

Scent trees before Jesus
evolution be a whole mess
of windswept dresses washed
up along the shipwreck don't you
know Tom Sawyer never left and still
painting the fence and the dope addict
brothers brawling and beating the shit
out of each other waking up the guests
at the charming bed and breakfast and
passive-aggressive mother whose husband
walked out on her for good reason and her
trying to break it up just trying to save the
precious antiques and the next morning
glaring at all the innocent honeymooners
just trying to mind their own business
the only time he be a tourist at the
quaint chalet in no man's land with
the grownup two-headed Siamese
twin always welcoming genuinely
glad to see him in perfect harmony
and a brand new inside joke told
to him in a whole incomprehensible
language but still able to understand
the pacing and rhythm and intonations
and naturally contagious and cracks up
like from all good slapstick comedians
with a sudden and awkward guffaw
as the vampire leads him to his bedroom
where a very shy and self-conscious parrot
with Tourette's Disorder who stutters does
the mantras in the corner and finally no one
knows him no one bothers him and left alone...

Never seem to leave well enough alone
that seems to be the whole Jesus thing
the whole cruel and brutal mankind thing
motif 'common' theme kit and caboodle
just hanging there on the cross hung-up
in days of Christ neither before nor after
neither when they invented B.C. nor A.C.
and then as the social workers so glibly
preach (to impeach or not to impeach)
just having the casual and
nonchalant ability to thrive
and get on with their lives
with their everyday
functioning daily rituals
and routines daily activities
as if nothing had happened
the fox giving birth
to a litter of triplets
in the pipes of
retention pond
where they keep
the dictator on-the-run
& kids from Vegas
& love letters
& bb gun...

He thinks being a crazy Jew would have loved to have been around during Nazi Germany and thrown out one of those mass follower Little Rascal high signs and then pet the little dick/tater on his head and go "O! He's sooo cute!" Chaplin did a good job imitating him too. He was a Jew think somewhere around The Midwest and of course good ol' original America ended up deporting him for their fear of him being guess something of a slapstick comedian and hanging out with the intellectuals and actors (those silent black & white home movies on the Hearst estate of San Simeon; very dangerous and 'threatening' crowd) and like those distorted mathematical proofs of the day and 'guilt by association' labeled him as something of a Communist. He thinks would have liked to have been branded too in the courtroom as something of a threat to our basic fundamental rights and freedom and an *Anti-American* and would have waddled in like Chaplin or that hobo or that douche bag Il Douche and played dumb and done his classic Italian accent "Scuze? No speeakee..." Guess Tailgunner Joe McCathy had no choice but through peer pressure of himself to deport him; what they did to Lenny Bruce just a decade later. Man I needs myself a bagel, matter of fact give me a dozen...

The decade following that of which we have never recovered they did a drive-by shooting on the Kennedy brothers and Martin and Malcolm

Still dusting for fingerprints...

He thinks...

I need Bessie Smith again
heart & soul & gut & groin
of good ol' New Orleans
I need the deep & dense
& distinct static of Satchmo
& Jimmy Rogers & Jelly Roll Morton
I need the sweating magnolia whose
semi-tropical melancholia never left you
I need the monsoons & screaming wind
through haunted shutters to the belfry
to the steeple to the cathedral of the mausoleum
I need to go back to the warm wonderful womb of Andalucía
composed of gypsies & Jews as if nothing ever existed
& have absolutely no need to ever return here again
I need to stray & sway in the shimmering bells of Brooklyn
I need Picasso's feminine svelte & rubenesque mandolin in
the pawnshop of the prison of the bizarre of his blue period
I need to slip like a madman into Magritte's illusions
I need to meet Edward G. Robinson & Orson Welles
the hero & hoodlum on the outskirts in the shadows
on the fugitive bridge on-the-run on the brink of film-noire
I need to meet weeping & wailing Jimmy Stewart after he loses
it all I need to eternally hug Kathryn Hepburn in the foghorns
turned to a ghost addicted to small talk & painkillers
I need to sleep forever in morphine & penicillin
I need that forest-green elixir from childhood which healed
ruminating & knew exactly where it was sitting in the clean
medicine cabinet I need to escape into the miraculous belly
of a firefly who suddenly shows up out of nowhere & blinking
beacon answers every cruel brutal question to why
I need to just join in in the symphony of peepers
who naturally materialize in the evening
in the swamp in the treehouse
in the moon in the stars
& ravage everything
every hypocrite every phony
every rabble-rouser every liar
of this supposed grownup world
in this obvious & predictable
trickery they refer to as living

I need to sleepwalk through this home
in this sin of a suburb in this obscene
act of a scene of a scene of a murder…

If think I because
Morgan from Oregon
where's my brown fisherman's
sweater from Ireland arguing
on how to get to Disney World
he pulls into the general store
to be miraculously cured
to hibernate in the shadows
for a little while to hope to
be reborn to go into denial
to be forgotten to be left
alone to be left with the old
mildewed unused aqua-blue
broken window doors leaned
against the shed to be no more
where they *do* sell tobacco to
minors and lotto and comic books
and dolls and cologne and cups
of hot steaming fresh coffee
to convince you to move on
beautiful young girls in their
tight teenager jeans to
attract and seduce
who come from
abusive households
looking to be rescued
and raise a family
of their own along
with a chicken and
a pig and a rooster
and a goat who also
come from broken homes...

Later on they will all go out for
live entertainment & cocktails
at *The Oriental Pearl* to try
and find a way of getting
along in this world...

The white chickens
& red wheelbarrow
glazed in rainwater
are gone missing
& the old retired
merchant marine
like clockwork
contented
disoriented
drags his wagon
full of a couple
cases of beer
through
the blizzard
of Brooklyn
the original
Hardy Boy
collection
each & every
one still stashed away
in the transcendent
soul of the attic
in one of those
ranch style
post World
War II homes
in Oceanside
Long Island.

Everyone has moved away
in mass exodus down to Florida
and that to him is the real disintegration
disappearance, and destruction of the
nuclear albeit extended family unit.

The greatest sprinkler system
was one of those little sprinklers
you'd attach to a hose and a whole
dead end full of kids, muted, who'd run
back & forth, fast-forward, in home movies…

In a place of non-belonging his dreams seem obscure symbols
and images and scenes of a 'distant belonging' but more so
obligatory and something he is supposed to believe and never
ever feeling particularly connected or comfortable with these
people, places or things nor really caring or wanting or desiring
what their illusory-like images with very little specific
or sincere or compassionate substance and meaning have
to offer and thus a very literal false sense of security perhaps
even a fear of intimacy if you will and thus these very concrete
yet perversely abstract and vague images and scenes of a
strange belonging only makes him feel more a sense of non-
belonging and thus one can eventually say his dreams of
belonging somehow through the opaque filter of his dream
world and sleep cycle become deep-seated feelings of non-
belonging excruciatingly lonely touching on his deepest and
most keen and profound fears of having absolutely nothing
no one nobody and inevitably resulting in becoming something of an eternal simple and spare nightmare always
appearing and feeling defensive and on-the-run and not
knowing where his home is which is exactly how he feels
out here not really being able to relate to anything or anyone
and contrary felt so much more a sense of belonging when
amongst the fleeting strangers and transient images and
constant state of flux and hustle and anonymity of the city
where ironically he never had dreams or for that matter the
need as the dreams out here in this queer artificial land of
make believe become a different kind of escapism only the
worst and most devastating kind like the kind he had as a
boy which represented and symbolized the fear of his parents
dying and going into a constant state of mourning and what
was to become of him and his life that death must be
something like this selfsame eternal constant state of
mourning or similarly like some dream or nightmare
that he cannot wake up from very much what he
feels out here alienated and alone...

While he's asleep
at night infomercials
come buzzing
for steam cleaners
& rowing machines
& blue topaz rings
what a weird
& distorted
version of
eternity
he thinks
(as if
touching
& teasing
& claiming
to heal & take
the pain & stain
right away right
out of his touchy
feely self-esteem)
Heimlich at last
finally resting
in peace

Resistance is futile...

They're starting to show those commercials
again for those coals which light on their own.

This is how America celebrates renewal
solstice for the new & improved season...

He prefers the early Seventies when they randomly
showed Broadway Joe with that *Listerine* smile
still in his uniform pushing a shopping cart
up and down the aisle of the supermarket...

That gigantic psychotic pitcher of *Kool-Aid* all of a sudden come to life crashing through backyard fences and scenarios of childhood surprising the neighbors to save the free world...

Juan Valdez picking each coffee bean one by one...

He thinks out here surrounded by all these false images
and phonies and liars like some absurd existential
joust with 'the nothingness' which of course would be
impossible to conquer and not sure he'd even want to...

The Spring makes him solemn...

He wakes up to an asylum of crows...

Shalom
Shazam!
Salam
Alakem...

And in/come into the dead end the home gymnasiums
& the landscapers with their thing-a-ma-job engines
& the portosans heading out to the parks and ocean
& the helicopters for the gangsters and traffic
& they're all these freeze-dried Caucasians
so fake & flagrant and this is what they
want & this is what they demand...

Almost burns the house down with latkes
and the gigolo firemen show up and comment—
"Do I smell latkes?" The blisters are starting
to heal. It's all a healing process and still
trying to get past the damage part...

He thinks he prefers homes so much more from a distance
not being able to see anything in them, nothing moving
just the shadows and silhouettes within, as when you
get to really know them, always prove to be such a bunch
of phonies full of hypocrisies and contradictions and become
a trigger to the trigger to the trigger to the trigger so moves
more towards the mythology and imagination of their
structure and placement, sort of like a museum
perhaps viewing transcendent exhibitions
and able to come and go at his own leisure...

He dreams of that long shadowy translucent home
where he used to read Dostoevsky all day long
a place where he felt safe to get depressed in
and a room with plenty of room to ruminate in
busts of African women he never experienced
but strangely used to brood about and imagine
with great big window and brook which overflowed
only time he felt he was able to understand and know...

It feels out here like these artificial (similar-like) structures
and forms (made to resemble, but opposite in feeling and
emotion) are the real life archetypal and mythological symbols
to a nightmare he cannot wake up from and the people (built
to-suit, built in suits) with their flat expressions and body
language and the repetitive way they function and judge
from their insular and ignorant (self-interested) worlds
there is nothing or no one real, which only contributes
to the real-life nightmare of which he feels so alienated
and alone and doesn't feel connected or comfortable
and never ever (deep down inside) wanted a part of...

He thinks how much a long time ago couldn't stand that inane commercial "Don't forget the zip code" didn't know what to make of it and what a weird sound to it *zip code zip code zip code zip code* how they prove you exist and how you get judged by your credit score your social security number your passport and your zip code…

He thinks all of that perfect landscaping has always kind
of freaked him out and frightened him eternally giving him
butterflies ironically making him want to flee always made
him feel excruciatingly lonely nauseated by the selfsame
need of its perfection and beauty almost in a sort of kind of
institutionalized and insular and sanitized and alienating
way somehow ruled by some amorphous and anonymous
big brother authority figure or sibling rivalry he knew he
could never trust and totally phony and fake and about as
judgmental and critical tyrannical and empty as its structure
and presentation and made him just want to race his bicycle
as fast as he could all that fear and isolation welling up in his
internal organs as if being trailed tailed by some nihilistic
phantom all the way home at sunset always seeming to
touch on the very fragile state of his being and mortality

Making it home just in time
for the church bells
and volunteer firemen...

He looks out his window to the numb flowers...

To the dandelion sun dropping in the bruised heavens...

Sitting at his desk as a child to do homework in his navy-blue Yankee jacket and canvas sneakers hearing the first rumbles of thunder like a stray visitor outside his window and filling up that empty dried-up brook giving it form and function now rambling like mad like some necessary redemption through the pachysandra to some holy and long-lost unknown destination...

Pigs sit under the bridge during rush hour to make their
quota when people are just trying to get to work just trying
to get home just trying to put bread on the table and will
literally plant themselves in a ditch on the side of the road
in the trees right outside toll booths right where commuters
need to just naturally try and pick up speed.

If The Dynamic Duo were around today they'd be sitting
in that camouflaged bramble of weeds inside the middle
of that plume of dusty smoke right outside The Bat Cave
when it opened up from the fantasy world to the real world
as the state cop all dressed up like a Nazi in his ten-gallon
and sunglasses and high leather boots starts to ask completely
innocuous and hypothetical questions trying to trip him up like
The Riddler and Batman with his head crooked all cocked
to the side like a confused dog goes *you know I really
can't tell you...*

He wonders why they refer to them as your honor
as from every judge he has ever encountered
in his childhood and adolescence and once or
twice as a grownup was so far from honorable
and just a joke and gave the impression like
you were taking up their time and going
through the motions and take a number
just like those cops who were the actual
provocateurs and acted like a bunch of
punks and thugs and tried to intimidate
you like a pack of harassing arrested
stage of development bullies leftover
in the schoolyard and had no
idea how to interpret the law
and here come the lawyers
playing good cop/bad cop
and those accused and set up
who got no idea what's going on
and once you escape 'the scene' and 'drama'
and get out of their grasp and control become
like Buddha wise one really knowing what it
is to suffer and 'that in a nutshell' is culture...

Why when you're always so tired at your wits end
your wife always asks you questions like should I
cut my hair and you're looking to cut your wrists
just lying there dead to the world with your face
down in the pillow like a cruise passenger washed
up along shore your kid humming in the tub and tree
frogs coming in; What again was that recipe for success?

Frogs legs on white bread?

Feeding green apples to the seagulls?

He wonders where did The Court Jester live
and was he ever an honored guest
at The Earlybird Special?

Did the queen finger herself?

What stage of evolution did the fireflies come in?

The wingspan
of JesusChrist
before he flew
off to the
heavens...

The pawnshops and boys howling at dusk humorous epithets
to the pretty young girls send me to the corner I've been bad!

Milfs with tight spandex on walk their tiny terriers
at sundown when boys return home in their pickups
to the farm and the embezzlers in foreign sport's cars...

A very demented version of war
of "This is what you're fighting for"...

Where did those great mythological heroes and warriors sleep the night before battle? At the foot of their wife's bed or wives at the foot of their bed? How to write a love letter...

Love is always having to say you're sorry...

Falling through not always a bad thing...

Faith is a glimpse between different forms
of having our freedoms taken away from us...

If only paranoia was a little more credible
always starts off so well (and real and
reality-based) and then ends like a bad
breakup with a dramatic borderline girlfriend
who you once very much cared for and loved
and ended in power-struggles and ultimatums...

He dreams...

In an o.c.d. kind of way
I want to go back to every
late-great naked girlfriend
I ever had every shape and size
every painted-on pained expression
every closed eye every issue and crises
every way they chose or chose not to live and die...

The pretty young girls along the shore do show off their fare share of feminine charm but in a subtle and classy manner, the angels of the fog, the blushing cherubs of the dunes, and in driving through the old lopsided weatherworn shacks and beach homes just trying to kill time to escape this life with his son when the dusk starts to warm up he naturally asks when are the huts gonna start popping up and he tells him I'm not exactly sure but a very good question...

4 ways I think therefore to prove I exist over Descarte's when asking 7 year old son to prove who he is...

1. i have curly hair
2. i have big blue eyes
3. i am not a zombie
4. i have a heart

1. he thinks why is the grand comparison always
i need that as much as a need a bullet in the head
(is that it? don't think it is) but if it is pretty lame
and obvious and yes i guess kind of accurate

2. those very demonstrative expressions
of porn actors like do they practice it?

3. the very precise drawings of diagram figures
like of gym teachers when they show the exact way
to exercise and lift a weight safely in the proper fashion

4. weird people just walking down the side of the highway
just for the sake of it and the aristocrats with their
mansions in the mountains ironically seeming
far more lonesome and distant

5. wandering great big immaculate supermarkets late
night beneath silhouettes of looming mountains and
empty strip malls and howling dogs and state fares holier
than cathedrals and feels far more connected with culture

6. tombstones after tornado

7. mulching the idols

8. girl scout cookies & whiskey

9. got to move my bowels

10. clean out bird houses...

10 Most Fraud-Stricken States
10 Most Fried Chicken States
10 Most Panic-Ridden States
10 Most Freud-Stricken States

"Can't seem to find my way..."

The conjugation of relationships...

Savior   Savior
Save her   Save her
Savor   Savor
Safer   Safer

How to live happily after ever...

1. plant a virgin mary in the mulch
2. put up one of those satellite dishes
like a tulip on the roof of your home
3. make sure the metal shutters and aluminum siding
perfectly match and are uniform like a sunset orange
or razzle-purple until it all looks like some
sort of sweet 16 cake or giant creamsicle
4. sit on your tractor with your light beer and sunglasses
pretending to be the perfect provider and father really
cheating with multiple women refusing to pitch in
5. separate the trash from the recyclables
6. separate the desirables from the undesirables
7. obsessively manicure the bushes and hedges
to death until everything looks perfectly immaculate
with one of those power tools like some electric knife
you'd use to separate flesh from bone
during the hi holy days of ho-hum...

He thinks of certain such things...

1. Who was that fucken genius who made up that expression
having something to do with the invention of sliced bread
as never got it and never been a big fan of sliced bread
and more preferred a nice baguette to pick at instead

2. Who the fuck in the board room
came up with that brilliant spiel
"Trust the Gorton's fisherman..."

3. Who was the first to say get off your high horse
and wonder if that happened anytime during
that period of The Napoleonic Wars?

4. What happened to that one don't be a Budinski?
That seemed to be pretty big in The Seventies...

5. What's the opposite of nope?
Hope? Okey-dokey?

   How his mom used to say that
   when she hung up the phone

   Used to think was a great non non-sequitor
   after like some seven hour long conversation...

Crucify me & stone me & leave my bones by the ocean
there are so many women I have fallen in love with

(They should drop a bomb on a police
precinct instead of an aspirin factory)

What is the greatest monster masterpiece?
I mean when they really used to make movies...

I never wanted to make anything of myself a matter of fact
confident I never wanted to make anything of myself and
could never picture or imagine exactly what that would look
like or that day or moment when I made something of myself
and always found myself very resentful and reactive and a
real wise ass to those who had suggested I make something
of myself as by looking at them and this is what it was
to make something of yourself I was confident and
sure I did not want to make something of myself...

He thinks...

My friend I grew up with I found out now wears Speedos
around the barbecue and invites over he and his wife's
friends to their pool. I could never quite get used to
the whole concept of growing up as it just always
seemed so crude or maybe just perhaps that was
just him that I could never quite get used to?

They gather in separate groups where the men talk about
all things mechanical and all the people they got working
under them, while the women go straight for the liquor
and wine coolers and get loud and try to get everything
out and everything out of them.

In that scenario I think I'd find myself getting attached
to the weather and walking home alone feeling
lonelier than ever with the leftovers...

He thinks if ever I should win
or am a contestant or runner-up
for The Nobel Prize for Literature
or The Nobel Prize for Psych 101
or The Nobel Prize for survival
& coping & defense mechanisms
in the face of a very offensive world
or The Nobel Prize for Abnormal Psych
(as a cure for the very normal life)
or The Nobel Prize for Phobias
or The Nobel Prize for Nightmares
or The Nobel Prize for being noble
or The Nobel Prize for being peaceful
in a classless culture which is disgraceful
or The Nobel Prize for best imitation of a human
or The Nobel Prize for winning The Nobel Prize
I want my picture to be of me just sitting there
on the potty in the morning staring in a glazed
daze out the washing room window like one of
those immigrants gazing through the submarine
porthole coming into the new world as whenever
I think back to this I mean the immigrants and all
think how much more I prefer the image and scene
of the old world and if there ever was the option
of a return ship back to the old world as appears
to me to be so much nicer and kinder and surreal...

He thinks out here all it really feels
like is some surreal dimly-lit tavern
with ambiance in the haunted inn
& the blind waiters & waitresses
& wind-up maitr'di with the whip
& the silhouette of dazed kids from
the institution staring through upstairs
rear staircase bed & breakfast windows
romantics come to life in the graveyard
fast food joints along the strip mall
like upside-down capsized cruise ships
suburban movie theater with long violet
elevator & soulless patrons who will
try to turn wanderers (hard-working
loners & scholars) into strangers
a stabbing outside the country club
dali-lamas being limoed along the ocean
the exhibitionist in the historical district
making a good living with tourists from
hell who still pretend not to see a thing...

Dreams of girl scouts with bloody fangs
flirtatiously showing up to his front door
asking for donations while their insane
mothers who haven't been touched in ages
stand in the distance at a distance angry and sarcastic
threateningly rapping brass knuckles into their palms...

Today saw a stoic looking older man with his shirt off
bronzed slight paunch drinking a beer from a clear bottle
right in front of a sign which simply read *Chimney Repairs*
think they were getting ready to put up the state fair and
dandelion ships were coming in with immigrants looking
to make no name for themselves and just to be left alone

He wishes to be strapped down to the *Good Ship Lollipop*
and returning to the old country they're always talking of...

The greatest criminals he thinks and knows for sure
are those who will try to steal your heart and soul

Your *spirit* from you...

Paranoia getting the better of him for good reason
very reality-based or based in reality when house
going into third *Dustyefskin* year on the market
and devils you get stuck with on a daily basis
and those who are supposed to be advocates
forced to have to put your trust and faith in.

Funny how the white devil can view one as a criminal
when they are the antagonizers and provocateurs and
historically (hysterically) and (non) spiritually based on
gossip and rumors while can be the nicest and kindest and
most generous and consistent. When they first moved out
there they came onto them (with their issues and previous
wars and battles and bad marriages) and for some sort of
'splitting' and 'overcompensating' defense-mechanism of
'reaction-formation' (a perverse or opposite-like psychological
phenomena where people will displace their hostile or passive-
aggressive energies onto someone, such as histrionically say
how much they love but deep down inside detest or loathe)

And the friendly (not so friendly) neighbors came onto them
swear from day one literally the first day that they moved in
couldn't even get their furniture in for purposes of alignment
(forming allies) while wasted and haggard wife next door
shows up out of nowhere with some sarcastic, pasted-on
smile staring his wife down 'cause she was so much prettier
and younger and what could she possibly be doing there?
A week before on this very exclusive cut-out cul-de-sac
dead end when he was just trying to set up the home the
association gigolo would literally just ring his doorbell and
could smell the liquor on his breath, not sure what he
wanted, like did he want him to be part of some he-man
woman hating club?

Like it was their job or role to be there to save (to serve &
protect) them; ode of the masses and the mediocre, of the
conformist and follower; of the nonbeliever, the classless
who ironically literally try to set up some mock class-system;
self-entitle people, places, and things with some ridiculous
made-up verbiage or lexicon as 'desirable' or 'non-desirable'
with their clinically narcissistic privilege and entitlement like

it is always some honor to be in their presence when
there couldn't be anything more average and obvious.

He and the wife had not changed one bit
since the first day that they had moved in...

Why he so often had to turn to his fantasy world and
imagination to a time and place (and period of hope
and innocence) when this shit never ever seemed to exist...

Feeling real down in the dumps wound up these days
he dreams of that female neighbor from his youth
in the suburbs just over the fence in his backyard
who was like best friends with his older sister
practically a part of the family he had heard
recently had something of a real bad marriage
and was eternally sad and in a dream suddenly
finds his hand beneath her sundress reaching
for her deep warm hairy pussy and she says
something along the lines but doesn't remember
exactly because it was the inflections and nuances
of a dream but the feelings of Joey don't or please
or why are you doing such things and me kind of lying
like I didn't mean but really did and in desperate need
and in a strange awkward mutual way falling in love
with each other and her creeping into the dark kitchen
to the refrigerator for a glass of milk and am like what
did I do now how did she fall in love with me my greatest
mistakes in life and in relationships was making moves
way too quickly getting myself into a hell of a lot of trouble
in the love game

Thinks it having a lot to do with the desperate need and
'reaching out' and how quickly something of simple beauty
and purity can so easily turn dirty and filthy but thinks more
accurately if I was really being honest with myself how in my
present day conflicts looking back to the innocence of youth
for guidance to try and be healed and saved by the opposite
gender yet in the long run being found out (by myself) in
some form or another...

He wonders if ever there was a secret agent who just couldn't
keep secrets who spoke from both sides of his mouth and
couldn't help being sarcastic who got sick of the business
and said shit like just call me Ralph and would hang out
in the pizzeria all day and order slices and become a staple
and watch the ballgame and couldn't get him to leave and
flirt with all the up and coming silly pretty girls of the
neighborhood making a complete idiot out of himself
during his staged arrested stage of development and
at the end of his long and hard unearned day return
home past the barber shops and bakeries to bring
a baguette and bouquet back home to his wife and
drink away the night from his supposed secret agent
pension or claims of being on medical leave with cops
showing up practically every evening with him either
slurring trying to charm them that being Ralph the
semi-retired secret agent bragging and boasting or
passed out on the linoleum dreaming his life away...

The season as always has suddenly secretly changed
and all the idiot neighbors like slaves are out there
on their lawns with their little sucking-up machines
he thinks the perfect scene for a drive-by shooting...

Can't believe in Mid-November still got the landscapers
out there? What the fuck they mowing? The shadows?
Or is it like some dumb version of the healthclub when the
stairclimber naturally slows down and reads "Cool Down"

Ironic always for the ones who are never out there
Waits for some package to be delivered by a long-lost friend...

The worst thing he thinks out here is to be understood
(or what they believe they think they know about you...)

He tells his wife he actually feels bad Burger King fell behind
and into third place in the fast-food wars or whatever they call
them as actually has good and decent memories and would
go there with his friends while they were flame-broiled and
remembers engulfing Triple Whoppers which would stay
with him for the remainder of the day and maybe just
maybe deep-down inside this touched on something
far more fragile like some kind of pure and naive
innocence that they couldn't keep up with them

Like feeling eternally left behind
always feeling like the best men...

He puts his homemade iced coffee down in the middle of her cell phone and sunglasses and denim jacket and she asks "Why you gotta put it down right there? You have a whole kitchen island to work with." "I just missed you, he quips." "O cry me a river separation-anxiety boy!" For some reason he always feels this way in the morning with his heart down to the ground and knows the only way to get out of it is simply sit on the pot with cool fresh air morning breeze rushing through the cactuses on the sill and into his lungs to wake him up. Some times the fish. He strangely enough in the moment starts to think back to all those mythological heroes in high school Hercules? Ajax? Atlas? Apollo? Who they were and what they did?

He thinks in looking back at old black & whites
of young girls and ladies like in The Fifties and early
sixties it almost seemed like from a guy's perspective
they made dresses out of the material they make curtains
and somehow in a perverse way things seemed so much
more interesting and mysterious like something was really
happening like when maybe fooling around and a whole big
heap of curtains just sitting there like a rumpled carnation
all bunched-up in a leftover clump by the foot of the bed...

He misses that summer simply surviving off the general store
off fresh-cut cold cuts and Vermont cheddar and Portuguese
bread and newspapers and intimate small talk with that red-
headed woman who was a wife and mother on the lake in
the wilderness and had a girlfriend on the lake as well who
worked as a groomer and he'd see her everyday at dusk
after grooming and do some of the best fucking ever
forgetting it all realizing there really was nothing to
forget at all in this lost and anonymous Summer
having absolutely nothing to do with anything
at all in that very fragile and forgotten world...

At night they'd just take drives and not say a word to each other just sounded better and drift through the mountains and misty pastures and old inns and graveyards with a box radio listening to classic Negro blues singers wailing their sorrows strumming guitars with bottle caps once cotton pickers from The Deep South...

He randomly starts to wonder what were his thoughts
returning home from bar-mitzvahs some time back
then in the back of his mother's car in the back
of his mind and his nice little knitted tie supposedly
having become a man very passionately and earnest
and sincere having danced the night away to *Disco Duck?*

Baby soothe my mind then dump me outside inside
the outside and instead of pouring malt liquor all over
me like the brothers which honestly would be just as fine
how about a little seltzer like those Zionists from that tiny
Israeli enclave of Manhattan right around *Tal's Bagels*
on Amsterdam and also in The Upper East Side...

He thinks he wants to convert from reformed Judaism
one day and climb the ranks like in The Cub
Scouts to Ultra-Orthodox

Then when he gets there put on a yarmulke
and whoever they are beat the tar out of him with
a kosher salami lot the way he's been feeling these days

Top it off with seltzer straight from the bottle
the way the real Jews did it
from The Lower East Side...

Out here he feels like a secret agent to a lost cause...

He breathes out loud *gosh!*
(Past tense of God)...

How he wants to be on suicide watch and stare right back at them and ask what'cha looking at and charm 'em like he usually does and ask if they want to maybe get a little take-out Chinese and knowing him being pretty schmoozy ask how's the family and giving them a pretty generous tip as always...

The phone rings and it's the asshole bozo Police Benevolent Association asking for donations and he thinks this pretty much takes the cake should he donate part of his paycheck for literal police harassment for all the silly shit like supposedly not making a full stop through a stop sign across from University of Massachusetts having used his intuition and instincts and proactively looking both ways and ticketing him for 125 dollars and when asking them what they're stopping him for literally doesn't know tell him they don't have to and they run the show then bringing in another trooper suspiciously looking in the back of his car and he's got roses from *The Home Depot* and a copy of The DSM-IV to diagnose mood and personality disorders and them throwing him to the ground in front of his home cause he told them he didn't want to sit down on his front stoop and preferred (I prefer not to?) talking while standing so the phone rings and it's pigs and punks and pussies from The 'Benevolent' Police association asking him for money...

He instantly for some reason thinks of the image of The Joker from Batman with that great big wide and psychotic smile crazy lipstick and guffaw when he thinks of this rapport...

He hangs up the phone...

In playing with the kids outside by the jungle gyms
his wife hears from the other wife next door—

"He's been in Dubai and Kentucky for two weeks"
They kid around they're probably happier
life & times of a chemical engineer

Wonders what his thoughts are on the way
to Dubai and Kentucky probably at a loss
only seeing the inside of hotels and airports

Pretty freaken Kafkaesque always
with some real life like illusory
3-4 hour delay in Newark...

All these ridiculous meticulous people obsessively working on their lawns in like radioactive goggles and jumpsuits are like the opposite of the vision of landing a man on the moon. She bends over to try and make her husband jealous but doesn't do a thing for him cause knows exactly what she's doing it for and feels worse off for him. The crazy kid comes around the dead end...

They get it looking great but don't pay any attention
to each other and she hasn't been touched in ages.
They did knock out the perfect quota of children
just exactly like their vision but in raking up
nature find more so simply get on their nerves...

She disciplines them by screaming down from the kitchen and through the garage doors to the monkey bars in the backyard. Is this what they mean by having a nice flow?

Everything on the dead end looks picture perfect but when really get close to it hear the perfect father with the perfect marriage (whose wife reveals how cheap he is and hasn't been touched in ages) hollering "Get dressed!"

To him seems something of a slow death sentence
with a couple celebrations couple balloons
hanging off mailboxes every so often...

The shadow of a hang glider straying
and he wonders how's the pilot doing?

Maybe thirty years later he still sees himself as a procrastinator whiz at detention wall. In the morning still has a melancholia finding it so hard to get rid of and that great big white oak which got knocked over the year before in the storm and has planted a crab apple in the windy part of the lawn watching it blow...

He looks out his kitchen window
and discovers kids play like butterflies...

Instead of that infamous Munch painting and don't mean
famous Thelonious Monk from uptown Harlem downtown
Haarlem wants to storm across his back porch and howl
not like Munch but more so Monk with the funk while
muted tears are rolling down his profile with shish-ke-bob
on the barbecue; thinks why guys stay away from wife's
girlfriends knows as well they can't keep up with them...

He thinks the blacks said it best (like they often do) and
thought of those expressions like "act like you know"
and "you don't know me like that" and "they started it
and we're simply ending it" and he feels caught without
rhyme or reason and having no choice in the matter
between act like you know and you don't know me
like that and of course in the long run final denouement of they started it and we're simply ending it...

What can drive one crazy are those phonies who are flaky with your fate. Never trust the lawyer, the real estate agent, those types who often live and naturally thrive by the twist of phrase and lie and really couldn't give a flying whether you live or die, unless of course they can make a buck...

He thinks back to adolescence and how much he still loves
Joe Strummer from *The Clash* who just said it all without
really saying it at all and wishes just once he had met him

How his anger was so on point, was so fucken accurate
and hit it right on the head, probably didn't even know it...

To never lose sight of the vision at the end of his dreams and never get caught up in all the bullshit in between...

He used to like the girls who would grab it like now they own it one of the few ways he liked to be controlled and taken advantage...

He looks back at some of those crazy relationships
like an almost necessary wild out of control abeyance...

Almost like an abnormal psych. class
the ones in which he learned the most...

He broods such true-blue thoughts—

The only thing I cared about as a teenage boy was
masturbation the only thing that seemed to make
any sense at all the perfect and pure liquid gold

Like some sort of miracle
that helped me to forget it all
as if nothing ever existed at all...

Wants to drown in a bottle or jug of really good bad
red wine and add ice to it even though I know you're
not supposed to but always do dozing off to one of
Jimmy Stewart's black & white film-noirs even
though I know it really isn't but always thought
of it that way if you really ever stop to think about it...

It is so funny. People end up respecting you
for all the wrong reasons and do the opposite
for whatever hackneyed and distorted (self-loathing)
bullshit belief they're projecting onto you until you
come to realize (probably realized a very long time
ago in your adolescence and youth) how obvious
and mediocre and shallow and superficial they
all are. And it is at that exact moment it hits
you at the dullest of times how deep down
inside (not very deep) what a lack of respect
(how full of shit) you really have for them...

It is so hard to keep up with the mediocre...

Whole life an eternal game of hide & go seek...

If it's all about perception
hate to know what
fucken reality is...

Wow certain shit that certain individuals believe
without ever having the ability or potential for
considering (or the free will and volition which
also is representative of ignorance, brainwash
and self-deprivation) of independent thinking
is also a lost and absurd way of *not* believing...

He broods & thinks—

People make me feel illegal
when I'm probably one of the
most honest people I've ever known...

People get judged on the shallowest of shit
ironically not by coincidence
by the shallowest shits...

Beware not so much in what and where and why
they try to hurt you but in just the absurd
and desperate effort in even trying to...

Anyone who tries to disempower you
through such tactics must be powerless
and an active as well as *inactive* disgrace...

They used to always say take a deep breath
but used to always resent clichéd shit like that
because what if you just couldn't even get to that...

Enough is enough with playing by the rules
when the people you know who make the rules
are a bunch of fools and liars and don't tell the truth...

People will make you feel like you are not real
and invisible and like you don't even exist at all
Funny, always comes from the most unreal people...

Why is it that it is always the phonies who try to give the impression they're living happily ever after?

More often than not 'the criminal'
had far more criminal things
done to him than you can
ever even begin to imagine
sometimes so consistent
and constant blocks
and doesn't (tries
not to) remember...

Often the witnesses and innocent bystanders are just as criminal if you observe and study and look at them closely or ever had the experience in being in one of those situations in everything they are so vociferously saying; vociferously not saying...

Dreams with their sudden flash clips and images often play wonderful games of opposites of the exact person you think you are as it's all the stuff you are hiding and compartmentalizing and suppressing for purposes of coping and surviving just to get on...

Who the fuck are The Jones' and who the fuck cares about The Jones'? And if it's all about keeping up with The Jones' and you catch up to them doesn't it all eventually end up amounting to nothing (something really empty) one big grand illusion?

It sucks having a sixth-sense
stuck in all this one-dimensional nonsense...

Sometimes feeling cursed is a way of believing in God...

Giving up on one's dreams is almost obscene
and the repercussions (believe it or not) deadly...

Wasp kills wasp...

(They drop names like expensive silverware...)

No love lost how could there be if never any to start off?
And will now fade away fucked-up keeping it all tucked
In all the gossip and rumors all the craziness and hurt
and pain all the sexual repression which never really
ever seemed to exist in the first place happily ever
after poised and perfect to the sunset...

He thinks to live and survive out here is the most absurd
and pathetic and futile example of some *death defying act*...

He asks where is my maid to change my sheets
and make those perfect little hospital corners
like Proust's nanny who used to copy over
all his drafts of *Remembrances of Things Past*
he drafted directly from his queen-sized bed from
the olfactory trigger of a certain brand of menthol
rub while breathing in and out having flashbacks
overlooking all of the spirits from the present and
past trying to keep up with the aristocrats of Paris...

He stands in the shower dead to the world
with his son's 3-d glasses on singing old Stones
songs—"I know you find it hard to reason with me..."

Thinks when Injun Jim went clattering through the courtroom
and leaped through the glass window to the grass way down
below to win his freedom being the self-fulfilling criminal

Living in the moment and on-the-run liberated
that that there is the psychological and social
and cultural and spiritual history of America...

How almost all of contemporary civilization
was built on some strange superstition

excluding the majority
and letting only a few in

To think almost all of modern society
was built on an 'absurd' delusion...

Eventually in postmodern American civilization
all you are going to see are candidates competing
going after each other on commercials on the t.v.
symbolic archetypal put-together product figures but
be like some eternal recurring Kafkaesque nightmare
where no one will ever win anything matter of fact
you won't even know what they are running for
and simply go back and forth forever and ever...

Today he goes out in the woods and they are shooting
and killing every *practical* living and moving thing in sight
(out of sight) couldn't get a moment's peace swear couldn't
even hear the birds or rustling leaves or wind blowing or
breeze (guess it was one of those allotted days like a Monday
or Wednesday or state cops getting in their quota) thinks in
America they do not allow you to think in America they tell
you not to think in America they demand you not to think in
America damned if you do damned if you don't if you try to
think in America the classic and literal cliché of if you can't
beat 'em join 'em so might as well which thinks and wants
you to believe we're so well loved and respected like some
abusive parent got you believing see-thru bullshit brainwash
machine then give you a couple of moments to maybe reflect
but beware not too long as don't want you to grasp or get it
lost somewhere between the murder and mayhem (this is
what they refer to in the commercials and news programs
of what makes America "great" still don't get that? How this
is historically what has always made us such Renaissance
Men and individuals and independent, yeah I guess they're
right if they're referring to carnage and bloodshed) and after
taking their much-deserved lunchbreak these o so brave
Elmur Fudd hunters (these state of the art state police
men well-sculpted from the gym who are more sinners
and criminals who will try to entrap and bully you) shooting
at the heavens these retired I mean retarded what they like
to do with their down time I mean their free time what they
like to refer to as male-bonding what they like to do to unwind
and then rewind when they're done with their sandwiches and
obvious jokes and punch lines reload the artillery and ammunition and *bam! bam! bam! bam! bam! bam!* never had a
chance on every living and delicate creature every beautiful
bird every singing specimen every deer who didn't make it
and won't be returning home to their family and the self-
entitled courageous All-American man returns in nice little
rubberized camouflage uniform and look-alike hats and boots
with their guns to their souped-up pickups to treat their
women like second-class citizens like they are invisible
and are not even there the mothers to their children

and treat their friends they grew up with even better
but it's all a part of the culture and got to learn
to live with it and not think about it and accept
it or become a victim...

In America these days seems like everything's based
on some statistic. Want to burn it turn it around
backwards upside-down to find the true core
image experience. Most of the people who
compile this shit and intellectualize it
have never come close to living it...

He thinks these feel days I feel no feel at all feel in jail
and no visiting no feel at all no feel at all and all those
little assholes moving their little pieces around just
happy to have my little peace of feel no feel at all
in jail feel no fail at all in jail am in jail and feel no
feel at all wouldn't you know couldn't be happier?

In these tourist towns they got liquor/wine for the grownups
and ice cream for the spoiled brats all to placate and sedate
and will live happily ever after in their dreams at *The Blue
Dolphin Motel* with h.b.o. and an indoor pool and if they
don't get these instant-gratifications they are miserable
and look to scapegoat and hate the world; the pale pasty
morbidly-obese kid with his gimmicks, the morbidly-obese
motorcyclist with his pre-manufactured anger all take off
from the fast food stand past the graveyard and competing
motels and mini-golf never seen from or heard from again.
The girls field hockey team sweeps in with their sandy-blonde
hair and long popsicle stick legs naturally seducing everyone
around them and even start in on the fathers and young men.
The international guests that being the Asians and those
from India seem like the best and the brightest and well
educated while Caucasians try to give off this impression
but just miss because with them it's all about control and
confrontation (an absurd competitiveness) and privilege
and entitlement and a real lack of suffering and experience.
It all seems like a really sad and pathetic and nihilistic version
of one's existence and triggers mortality in all the worst and
most sleazy and shallow and superficial of ways and wish
and dream for something as far away from places like
these and he just wants to flee and hit the road again.

He imagines Jesus got his start somewhere around here
strapped to the cross like a piece of shish-kebob
and paraded down the strip mall...

Cop in cop car literally planted in forest
(like some weird and fucked-up fairytale)
right across from the *Tasty Freeze* and what
they're waiting for he knows not what but...

He thinks of Jesus
and that moment
on the cross and
if it ever once
crossed his
mind in a
flashback
to fight back
a surreal
nightmare
which will
one day be
worshiped
and revered
and adored
a little kid
with marbles
and slingshot
plays with
magnifying
glass and sun...

This morning his kid senses he's feeling a bit blue and down in the dumps and drained and fed up with life and tells him to go in his rocking chair and puts his super hero blanket over him and all his stuffed animals (suppose to make him sleep better) like some great big empty hollow Buddha with trinkets and jewels hanging off him and tells him to go to sleep then puts in *Yellow Submarine* very good soundtrack to put in when you're feeling blue and down in the dumps and fed up with living you know "Hey bulldog, Eleanor Rigby, they'll screw you in...and fill you with their sins..." and while he's napping his son is drawing as he's been grounded from t.v. and when he awakens makes him a cup of hot chocolate and a peanut butter and jelly sandwich and thanks him while invisible rain starts to come down in the paint-by-number forest...

There's a farmer who lives in the front of the cul-de-sac
with his tiny little house and chimney and plot of land
and seems as content as ever before there ever were
any of these cul-de-sacs and all this crap which leads
to more crap and more crap and more crap and more crap
and he seems to just keep himself busy and mind his own
business with his daily tasks and whenever you pass him
and leave the cul-de-sac with his great big flower garden
of statuesque roses and gladiolus and other such assorted
prickly things and his knocked down trees and tree trunks
and clotheslines can't begin to tell you how envious or
perhaps rather more accurate just how much respect...

So once again he turns into the trails in the back of
his backyard to get away from it all and ironically feels
so much more familiar and calm (at home) then suddenly
stares through the deep trees of the dense forest at the
illusion of the perfectly immaculate man-made lawns
in some cul-de-sac of a suburb as if knowing it all
looking backwards through the keyhole like some
really fucked-up dysfunctional Monopoly board
with a bunch of really bored and filthy and vulgar
uninspired actors going through the motions playing
unconvincing roles and within this perfect mirage and
scenario perversely knows and feels and has experienced
so much more conflict and confusion and contradiction
than anyone could ever possibly imagine. They are
a trigger to all his worst possible emotions and their
homes stand like monuments like mausoleums like
mediocre museums like manicured pyramids to
worship their own pathetic pimp prophet existences
of a fragile feeble mean-spirited Napoleonic demeanor...

Fact so much stranger than fiction
but out here from a Kafkaesque point of
view and position there is no fact because
all a bunch of fucken liars and hypocrites...

Being in some sort of eternal and existential prison of which he has been granted parole and has been told he can go based on paying his dues and good behavior but they have no place to put him...

Forced to waste away with all those miserable sexless ladies from the Marx Brothers comedies and their slave masters without a sense of humor or honest bone in their body...

He thinks how he's got absolutely nothing to say
to any of these people any of these fools trying
so desperately to act secretive and exclusive
but once they do, give away all their secrets
probably not too interesting in the first place...

Some carbon copy of an original probably wasn't particularly
original anyway trying to imitate some principle or ideal
from the *How To* section of 'How to Win and Influence'
really turned to some diluted form of aggression
and arrogance and ambition and abuse...

He thinks to himself there can be no worse thing
than to be judged by those who don't know a thing
about me (don't know a thing about themselves...)
small-minded and petty even delusional and distorted
in their thinking who don't have an ounce of experience
and haven't seen a thing who don't have an ounce of the
kindness or charm or compassion or generosity respect
or dignity or insight or being...

Thinks I think they should post and line up
some of the mean miserable bitches who live
on our dead end with their flat affect and dull-
eyed expressions and pass their parasitic gossip
and rumors cause no one looks at them anymore
and can no longer seduce as if they ever could
as to me philosophically and spiritually are truly
some of the biggest murderers, rapists and criminals
who ever walked the face of the earth and thrive off
being malicious and mean-spirited to others in order
(out of order) to function; Call it Dostoevskian but
man I'd love to see them all fucken lined up in there
when I go to pick up my stamps and thinks hell yeah
finally at last would be the perfect payback poetic justice
with all these disgruntled witches and bitches grouped
together (exactly how they're already configured)
the distant and dazed and dead exactly what they
phenomenologically tried to do to others and
now the zone and the town and the suburb
may be properly warned and these are
the real people you should keep your
kids away from so as to avoid any
sort of spiritual or psychological
damage or harm or scars or
brainwash profound feeling
of constant loss for the rest
of your days your life long...

When they push your patience and tolerance to that breaking point when you see (through all...) that they're trying to play games and showing absolutely no respect for you at all (which in truth characterologically and psychologically when you analyze and assess it showing really no respect for themselves and the features and signs and symptoms of a pretty weak and fragile identity and ego manifesting itself in episodes of self-interest and little pussy bullshit explosions and inconsistent and contradictory erratic moods and behaviors which often will manifest itself in abuses of power) you got no choice but to flip the script and teach them a lesson they aint never gonna forget and find out right there and then in the here and now (what they're all about) and don't know a hell of a lot about themselves and then their see-through tactics and games and patterns are not quite as quick and slick (not talking all that shit) as they thought they were and all all of a sudden want to be humble and best friends with ya...

Out here it's who can do the best acting
but they're not particularly good actors
all pretty much repeating the same lines
with the exact same affectations and look
bland and stale going through the motions
ironically perversely much more the audience
than any sort of actor (tourists and false witnesses
and fake players) looking to engage and engross
themselves into other people's drama (their bad
karma, extension to their denial) so as to deflect
and make their lives seem a little less miserable..

Out here they try and inject you with miserable mediocre
doubt or as the American Indian said the white man will
try to confuse and not too ironic when you turn the tables
on them and fuck them up and give them a taste of their
own medicine classically with their phony baloney character
and demeanor act like and literally use words like "I'm just
trying to be a good neighbor" with their convenient disconnect
and got one of the worst reputations for passive-aggressive
behavior and paroxysms and lies and double-talk and
ignorance and hatred and then interestingly develop
that selfsame character of the devil doubt that they
so nonchalantly tried to inject in you and act confused.

To overcompensate all their lies and hypocrisies and to feign
virtue they turn their lawn into a glossy picture perfect
postcard to be viewed by the rest of the false followers
of the fucked-up phony evil tourist choir...

Thinks...

I wish I could write a poem about America
in which I could express how much I felt
on a daily basis so goddamn displaced
and alienated and just not and never
been a part of and then saw this very
slick and earnest piano man with his bald head
and silk threads playing like some tragic melodramatic
Christopher Cross or Barry Manilow song in the middle
of The Warwick Mall with the wife and kid and thought...

Very sane madmen were walking in and out of the doors
single-minded and determined as if they were on a mission
but had forgotten the ammunition, while eternally angry
hateful fathers were staring you down inside theme
restaurants something the cookie-cutter Caucasian
out here appears to have the compulsion and culturally
likes to do and then when he saw me walk out with my
beautiful kid for some odd Dr. Jekyl & Mr. Hyde reason
decided to smile as if in some ridiculous senti/mental
alpha-male man-made way wasn't able to make
the connection between father and son

Think the piano man said he offered
private lessons and does bar-mitzvahs...

Always disturbed me deeply
that there weren't more
meltdowns and break
downs from the freaks
at the circus that they
didn't rise up completely
decked out in costume
and in raucous rebellion
perhaps even a punchline
of whispers a switchblade
or silencer to the brain
of their barkers maybe
even subtly sign
or inscribe
their initials
in a ceremony
of seagulls spit
on them and wish
them luck and push
them off through the sludge
through the carnations & needles
& rubbers to meet their makers

Will be the best Coney Islands
and onion rings they ever tasted...

Fuck this culture!
And why does it always seem
they're offering you something
you're not even asking for after
being on the road for god
knows how long? Why
we relate so well to Clint
kicking the shit out of
the whole evil posse
when all he's ever
done is mind his
own business
not wanting
to be bothered
to just get back
to that claw
foot tub
to soak his
tired bones
for a shot
and shut
eye and
maybe
a cat
nap
and
a cat
to shack
up with...

Remembers every year once a year his best friend who was
one of the biggest delinquents you'd ever want to know but
about as nice as they come and just couldn't control his
passion and anger and dad a brain surgeon how his pals
from Canada would just suddenly show up like the wind
in one mad drunken fell swoop coming down to New York
never quite knew how he knew them and what was their
relation and like some insane reunion we would all get
ourselves into heaps of trouble like buying bb guns from
the mall and like a bunch of half-crazed out of control wise
ass assassins with windows from his home half-cracked open
and while in other rooms wrestling and playing video games
with younger brothers playfully kicking the shit and torturing
each other would shoot at cars rounding the corner and
watch whole windshields gradually shatter then light and
ditch and take off to the forest and cops would show up
and his younger brothers would innocently help them to
retrieve and find the bb, get into stilly and stupid rumbles
in the back of movie theaters because we were sure kids
from rival towns were staring at us wrong and that weird
and absurd tradition of having to take off our t-shirts and
watches right before the movie began usually films like *The
Goonies* or *Ghostbusters* or some new James Bond smelling
Nathans and *Hunan Garden* just down the avenue, how we got
there racing down the highway and those crazy cousins from
Canada like a bunch of madmen would literally change seats
while they were driving and yeah so I really miss those times
and never quite sure what relation they had to each other but
used to love those bizarre half-crazed annual get-togethers
where all in good fun just couldn't turn down
a challenge and keep ourselves out of trouble...

Anti-revelations after contract ended for tutoring
out in the Bourne school system and hopping
on the treadmill for midday news...

Miss New Hampshire arrested for punching kicking scratching
and biting her boyfriend after he took away her cell phone...

Apparently her crown was taken away as well...

Year after The Royals got married
supposed to be like real people...

High clouds and winds for your
ballgame today out in Fenway...

Iridescent leaves from the pear tree start to flutter
outside the window and know the rain's a comin'...

His favorite part of that classic *The Graduate* when Dustin
Hoffman goes back to Cal. Berk for Mrs. Robinson's daughter
and she claims that her mom said he raped her when of
course she seduced him and he tries to explain it to her
and she freaks out and faints and he gets thrown out
of the boarding house based on the notion that he was
the aggressor or how they so-called liked to call it in The
Sixties 'one of those agitators.' After she comes to she calmly
asks him what he's gonna do now and with shaving cream
still on him stunned and dazed and numb wiping a little off
leaving a little on in that mental state and final denouement
of I just don't care anymore says—'You have to stop asking
me these questions' and this is what thinks a lot of what life
and existence is misinterpreted and underestimated by all the
wrong people (people he cannot relate to and has no respect
for) the adult world and blind masses when really a romantic
and passionate and that image of that leftover shaving cream
unshaven, defeated, determined, still blindly, bravely, barely
hanging on, holy, halfway haunted, heading towards
instinctive do or die destination...

The fate of the solitary 'stranger,' caught and stuck, fucked,
inevitably lost between cultures and systems and life stages
of growth and development...

Now even to be viewed with 'suspicion' and something
of a 'villain' with a pained smile and ripped wedding
dress on the back of the bus

All the muted shocked old timers just turned around
checking them out, the cross he used to fight them
off just to beat out the crucifixion climax...

Moses passes Jim and Huckleberry Finn moping
on their raft to the draft of burning incense and
cigarettes passing what's that? Roman Coliseum?
Eiffel Tower? The Chrysler Building? Babylon?

It's all irrelevant as always hazy and overcast
taught to mind your own business...

He wonders if ever there were birds who were born without vocal chords sitting out on the branch and crowing and wailing away all day long and thinks this is a breed I can definitely trust and believe in...

The crickets which start up at the back of the drive-in...

Would have loved to have been there
when Socrates was whispering
his words of wisdom to Plato...

What it means to be pleasantly stranded
(abandoned, blessed, and wounded)...

Suddenly realizes it's all one big cruel absurd high school and why even back then had absolutely no one to relate to...

Why he relates so much more to nature
and the change of seasons...

He dreams of changing his old realty agent as she doesn't do shit for him and trading her in for this new and improved and inexperienced one and knows she will work hard for him and dreams of inviting her to the woods to take strolls as they have always had a good rapport and fondling and making out with her and breathing new life into him...

His cock aroused
taking cat nap
in the middle
of the day
dreaming
of that young
blonde waspy
realty agent
showing him
that secret
rental
over
looking
the bay
and her
doing her
fair share of
post-collegiate
post-coitus
flirting
pulling up that
pretty little print
sundress of hers
only to discover
pulling down
those panties
an already nicely
prepared warm
and damp
moist pussy
taking her over
antique bedframe...

The old farmer who lives over the stone wall
way before any of this ever existed before
way before any of these people any of these
know-it-alls and suburban homes the only one
in which he has any real rapport tells him all
about his bluebird home and that he should
clean their nest out every season and keep
it plenty far away from his home and face
it east and they will come back in droves...

They just talked about all the buzzing nighttime creatures
and recent massive mass of fireflies and the coyotes
and wild domestic dogs from neighboring farms
who go back and forth in a choir under the stars
and then just naturally lit up a cigarette and smoked
it by his pickup and it was all cool and all good and felt
like no one or nothing could possibly bother them anymore...

Really knows the lay of the land and across the land
used to lay this old man from West Virginia who used
to literally live in a log cabin and spend his days whittling
sculptures to attract snowy owls and now lives this awful
horrible little leprechaun Lilliputian of a man always mad
and glares and having his mini meltdowns and explosions
and snap crackle pop paroxysms in a land of his own in his
own little bubble and actually a life insurance salesman
ironically paranoid and annoyed and terror/tory/yawl
acts like he's the one and only only one who lives there
and everything revolves around his American Dream
becomes everyone else's nightmare with his chainsaw
and lawnmower and leafblower trying to be all
aggressive and competitive and must one up
and control his neighbor at all costs with
the classic bullshit Caucasian excuse
that he's doing it all for his son
really an extension of him...

He thinks of that game they used to play opposites
and that it feels like the whole Caucasian culture is
always obsessively bent on trying to play opposites
trying to act better and more exclusive but when
you really get down to it when you really ge
to know them or their culture or where
they're from there couldn't be anything
further from the truth and realize none of those
games really matter or is relevant because deep
down inside find how homogenized and cookie
cutter like trying to all act and be exactly alike.

Who was it Plato
said it's all about forms
well couldn't agree more
or more so disagree more…

He retorts those truly 'suspicious' are perversely the insular and ignorant (turned dumb and defensive) who have never left their natural or not so natural environment, still trying (from a distorted perspective) to cop a demeanor of privilege and entitlement, making all these efforts to alienate others from their environment (when it's not even their environment to make such judgments and literally could not be anything less accurate or further from the truth because all they do is take and do not contribute with an attitude like everyone is there just to serve them) while ironically never even thought of them at all in the first place, white man's version of suspicious, absurd and ridiculous, what they cannot possibly control or keep down (fathom) in their rigid and delusional, closed-minded environment, and when you look closely, real closely, do a close-up of the close-minded clone, the filthy and vulgar 'ugly tourist' and 'not so innocent bystander,' see the one who constantly takes and does not sincerely contribute or offer something positive to the culture; the one truly to be held under scrutiny and 'critically' judged as 'suspicious'...

Likewise he thinks why is it always those who do all the laughing are the ones who haven't contributed particularly much to society? Maybe a couple materialistic items for themselves here and there which in his opinion doesn't really seem to add up or amount to a whole hell of a lot...

Turns out the people next door who had swatches
of different colored paint on the front of their home
the whole summer are ending up painting their house
the exact same color; the husband he thinks is some sort
of civil engineer and wife works in the financial department
of a hospital, and even asked guess 'cause she thought he
had class what color they thought they should paint it and
like always went out of his way to offer them his recommend-
dation, and just like everything else out here went with the
exact same drab color they had before like dreams that got
lost and don't exist anymore only to make sure they are able
to keep everything perfectly on the straight and narrow and
organized and safe and secure; He even went out of his way
to tell them when they inquired what color he'd paint the door
and had the place looking all brand new and gorgeous, but
again, just like everyone, just like everything else, nothing
out here surprises him anymore (never has and never will,
which is the whole damn, futile, pathetic, existential tragedy
of it all) thinks if had a little dough saved up would go out
every weekend and climb into one of those great big hot
air balloons with no return ticket home...

What is the final sound of the coyote
before he returns to the unknown?

He feels so alone sitting alone in the park in the drizzle watching his son on the jungle gym literally wedged between the graveyard and this girl riding her horse high up on horseback; Supposed to be the good part of town but couldn't feel more let down, (home)sick, claustrophobic and less culture, and not sure if it is conscious or deliberate brainwash (and knows it is not, just people trying too hard to play roles and wears on you and ends up just feeling bored and so alone) has found absolutely no one he can connect to or relate to; Funny, he grew up a white boy (wonders if he missed that class where they taught you to be arrogant and aloof) now amongst *killcagians* got absolutely nothing to say, wouldn't even want to who all strangely believe from a distorted point of view it's some honor to be around them and better than everyone; why it's ironic and the perfect metaphor, just sitting there all alone in the park in the drizzle between the graveyard and this higher than holy girl riding her horse high up there high up on horseback...

Dreams of maybe moving to one of those homes
where they murdered someone and there was
blood everywhere and don't disclose or tell
you somewhere on the border of Maine
and Canada in the middle of nowhere
kind of in the beauty of no man's land
as think they might offer it at a reduced
price and lower the taxes with price
less views and seems as though
in that true-blue scenario always
got something to look forward to...

He dreams of burning his house down to the ground
thinks that might just be the catalyst to get these
motherfuckers around (*very motivated seller*)
all these new-found HGTV experts to start
making offers and they'd go back and forth
making counter-offers while the flames
started crackling and licking and
being thrown all over the place

Humble owner just wanting to move on
and the know-it-alls, as when burning
to different levels and forms do their
comparative analysis and lowball
offers until it's finally sold...

Some golden spider has started to spin a magnificent web under the lamplight of his home and whenever he goes to sleep and sees him up in the corner of his vestibule it brings him great comfort and solace in the moment and the only thing he cares about like a solitary prayer and when all those asshole white devil stingy Caucasians are making their corny counteroffers on his home trying to squeeze every last thing out of him going back and forth for baseboards and washer and dryer and tree house and first born and heart and soul and ashes to ashes and dust to dust he'll just say "yeah motherfuckers take anything you want but we're keeping the magnificent golden spider web whether you like it or not! We're taking that with us!"
p.s. maybe also as well the rabbits and the rabbit hole…

Coming out of the much needed trails he sees his son's
Superman comic cracked open in the back seat
of his car which simply reads *Thwaaack!*

He wishes he had one of those Wonder Woman truth lassos
for all the lunatics and criminals and would just lasso them
up in one big massive ball like pulling fish from the ocean
and chuck them in the back of his truck while they were
still talking shit and gabbing their gums then transport
them to the local dump where they like him and got
big-ups as bullshits with the best of them and always
quick and clever conversation and genuine and when
the holidays come in always leaving them something
nice like a bottle of wine or whiskey or box of oranges
his relatives sent him up from down in Florida and while
he's standing over that little crushing compactor kabob
hearing their bones pleasantly cracking he thinks of that
Louie Armstrong song what a wonderful world it would be
then returns home to his easy chair by the screen window
which picks up the breeze dozing off in the corn...

Who cares about the sports scores?
How the weather man gets it wrong half the time!

Know when the rain's coming
tulips right on time...

He thinks in the fog how the grapes must be growing...

How he is able to relate so much more
to those lost out at sea...

He thinks how he never wanted any advice
in this life but just a little help...

Somewhere between the minnow
in the mud and man on the moon
is this strange thing called self...

Sometimes he realizes
it's not language at all
or language that will
guide or get him
through but body
language like an
old man simply
waving his hand
in the direction
of the infraction
of all that's bad
going "Ehhhh!"

Madman just sad man
wanting to be heard
and sick of holding
it all in (the repetition)
from bad man (and his
fake roles and reputation)
getting way too much credit
than he deserves getting it in
all the wrong ways when madman
once very good man who trusted
and believed (with even a sweet
demeanor) somewhere got taken
advantage and betrayed coming
from very modest and humble
origins and beginnings...

Lovers
are like killers
and vice versa
taking down
so many
with them
he loves
the change
of seasons
the scent of
chimneys
and wisps
of wild wilderness
the strange eternal
smell of magnolia
and cigarette smoke
and moonlit musty
covers of motels
which seem
to trail
up and
down
the east
coast...

Crow flies back and forth
from branch to branch
in front of window

What'ya know?

There's a new sign posted
in front of the courtroom
in Fall River which reads
something like "Pajama
Bottoms Not Permitted"

He used to drink all day after school cough medicine
in his bomb shelter bombed-out and dozing off
to Dostoevsky and The Doors till he was sure
he was good and gone and safe and secure...

While going into trees he comes upon a new and sudden
psychological hypotheses and theory and thinks one day
will write an essay on it on how all our truly profound and
significant and meaningful relationships existed with a real
and complete and deep mutual sense of honesty and integrity
and true fairness and being way before that period of natural
conflict and betrayal during the phase of puberty going as far
back to our childhood and adolescence from the ages of 3-13
and we more times than not always appear to look back and
reflect not out of coincidence but natural and transcendent
soul-searching and spirit to that instinctive and innocent
period some time during our later adulthood with a rich
and lucid sense of pure and pristine fondness and magic
and imagination that can never be penetrated...

He thinks the woods the only place he can
go the only place he can naturally escape to
where he does not feel judged and the deeper
he goes the more he explores its natural shapes
and forms its natural cadences and rhythms
the more that eternal and unconditional
feeling of love as if none of these
things had ever existed before...

What it means to really exist without the law
all those false and absurd and satirical abuse
of powers from the fake gods down below...

Counter-transference from all the clones...

(A psychological term in how he was trained
of what you represent to them and what they
project onto you without them even knowing)
yet somehow pretending to know it all when
he's seen and done and been through so much
more and wonders if there's some sort of Last
Tango some Last Waltz or one of those Electric
Slides he picked up during the stage of disco
to slip out and get him the hell out of there...

Why he goes into the woods: to go all out and do good
they always looked at him like he was up to no good
he likes that up to no good to go all out and do good...

Thinks all he really needs cup of coffee
and sun glistening off damp
leaves in the morning...

Dreams of one day being reincarnated
just being a part of that great big
bulbous beehive which latches
itself way up high in the holy
pines as if eternally hanging
up a do not disturb sign...

Of going into the trees all he needs
all he doesn't need is an acoustic guitar
couple bologna sandwiches and Scooter
Pies hearing the crazy dogs barking through
the pines those crazy old time station wagons
log homes with Howard Johnson colored shutters...

The awkward and romantic good looking high school
boys and girls making out in the woods and sometimes
even more with those secretive and sacred smiles the only
place they can escape to and who can think of a better place
than deep within the trees in nature in the trails where no
one can find them always with hickies in the exact same
area like proud trophies that they have earned and with
great diligence and determination worked so hard for...

He thinks in the trails of suddenly finding and meeting
that one beautiful mad stranger who will place some
fantastic romantic kiss on him and vice-versa
which will allow him to move on...

There will be absolutely no implications
(why should there be?) as if nothing
had ever existed before...

When it really comes down when there's finally at last no one
around he dreams of taking her to that great big greenhouse
that warm and humid and fragrant and exotic room and take
her from behind take her behind and open her up like a sticky
stamen sticking his rock hard thing into her willing and
welcoming lonely solitary pussy and like everything else
in this hot peaceful beating stirring jungle pollinating and
germinating and bringing everything back to life when all
you hear and all you see are shadows of that thudding rain
pelting and pounding and dancing and drumming up along
the long slanted ceiling and able to block out everything
as if nothing ever existed before no people no pain just
the sound of the rain and of beatific being and nothing
blooming and then simply disappearing like a couple
strangers who never met before like those blissful
birds that come out after the storm and naturally
pick up and scavenge all the leftover folklore...

Last red geranium of the season
still blooming like a live skeleton
like constant welcoming receptive
vagina you been recently missing...

When he walks out
through that space in the stone wall
he hears himself singing the Bowie song—
"God knows I'm good, God knows I'm good, God knows…"

He broods—

Does existence exist?
Does any of this exist?
Does desperation exist?
Do you exist? Do I exist?
I have loved every girl
I have ever been with
for reasons neurotic
and nihilistic and
seen so much
of me in them
(it's not even
funny) without
even knowing it
turned to wishing
and worship and
of course always
ending up being
those really tragic
melodramatic
breakups
and splits...

It's of this excruciating loss and damage
where he always strangely enough feels
the trigger to a very specific spirit of which
he can't quite explain nor would he even want to...

A team of wild turkey go flitting through the shadows of the trees in the woods and cross the road then just hang out on some postage stamp suburban front lawn and when they're there strangely enough look like they got nothing to do and nothing's going on but when they were trampling through the woods just a moment ago...

Returns home and simply looks out the garage doors
where he keeps the wise men and scarecrow
back to the Monopoly board and says
aloud to himself "Don't lose it all…"

Just put me out on the porch like some leftover pumpkin and I'll gladly live happily ever after like the barely visible holy tree frog propped up there surveying contemplating and ruminating and reflecting about the previous season and the chilly Autumn rolling in just around the corner...

Bluebird returns back to bluebird box
in the swamp just brooding up there
something he knows so much about...

All the recorders and rattlers and rubber duckies seahorses have all been cleaned in the dishwasher...

A bottle of baby bubbles between the spindles and when the sun reflects off it at day's end through the foyer window this simple and spare image just makes everything better...

Mickey Mouse holds onto toothbrush in toothbrush holder like some sort of harp or fiddle the only thing that means anything to him couldn't care less who's watching him...

At night when he raids the kitchen he has visions of stabbing his realty agent over and over and over again with a kitchen utensil preferably a fork right in the neck which takes some pressure off him and when she's dropped dead right there dead on the spot see if she bleeds or not like one of those *Stepford Wives* and thinks what would you call that? Pride of ownership? A motivated seller? Perhaps it might finally motivate her and get her off her flabby ass to try and sell this goddamn house after he practically kept her daughter out of jail by writing a letter to the judge after knocking off a gas station on the corner to get her fix when working at *The Moby Dick Methadone Clinic* against the policy and better judgment and consent of the clinic going way past the call of duty and not in the job description and being lovely human nature and full of shit still never getting a simple thanks or even making much of an effort and maybe with her dead on the floor bleeding or not with a fork in her neck might inspire this motivated seller to get granite or stainless steel appliances the new trend of the day of what the very "desirable" "family-friendly" population of Caucasians seem to be craving...

He humorously thinks maybe like that home
he and his wife saw in Upstate New York
he'll put a chicken on an electric rotisserie
spinning there right in the middle of the kitchen...

In the constant and continual counteroffers sending
contractors over to his home getting radon tests done
without approval the recent divorcee who still needs to
get approval from the courts to move her twins out of state
counters as if she was still involved in this divorce case
he must take down the tree house get new baseboards
and gets the tall barroom stools around the kitchen
island. He counters that she cannot have his bar
room stools as they are his and will only knock
down the tree house and get new baseboards
once the full and final purchase and sales
agreement has been signed. Turns out
the courts did not give her approval
to move the twins out of state
and ended up renting for a year
and the tree house stayed up
and the baseboards and the tall
barroom stools around the island

Kind of why he was not so quick to act
on her demands as saw this happening

Something he learned a long long time ago...

He sits there with his eyes closed by the seashore for god
knows how long with the home inspectors traipsing through
his home and lord knows who else maybe his realty agent
and attorneys and contractors and witnesses and assassins
and priests and rabbis and caterers and third grade teacher
and with his eyes still closed shut tight sees two beautiful
young pretty Asian girls stroll by with their expensive
cameras and thick sunglasses and safari hats and grins
and while he's conked out there they pick up a rock and
conk him over the head until he's good and bludgeoned
to death still with those same demure grins on and he
goes down like a fine wilted dandelion who's lived way
past his time and lucky cause doesn't have time enough
for his life to rush in front of his eyes and does hope their
shots came out well and honestly does wish them the best.
When he's literally dead to the world having also somehow
developed and picked up their smiles he hears the circus
caravans casually rattle by with all the circus animals
taking in the lovely scents of the seashore to catch
a breath of fresh air...

Recently he's been having this violent fantasy of strolling
with all the bad realty agents he ever knew into the dunes
and pulling down their pants and giving them a spanking

they aint never gonna forget than blasting—"Go to your
room!" and them just silently turning around blushing
bowing their heads and disappearing out to the ocean

He sighs like a fire engine going out to its fire

Dreams of getting caught in the downpour
of his backyard porch and praying for...

He wonders when John Coltrane started using dope...

All he ever cared about the crashing shore knowing that
it will constantly repeat itself 'till eternity and this makes
him feel more safe and secure always has and always will
sound of syllables coming in from the deep ocean and the
repetition of that motion and still haven't caught up to him
like the good old Birdman of Alcatraz and Papillion played
by Steve McQueen taking a great flying leap one giant step
for mankind from the precipice of Devil's Island into the
beautiful and blissful final unknown of the Mediterranean
and never seen from or heard from again but as the captions
or closing credits imply somehow did survive the fall and swim
and to have lived out the rest of his years and life in freedom

From experience he knows this is the only thing
that really matters as simple as that of which
most people have no concept about...

He and his wife take off for the weekend
to try and make it all work for them...

Finds himself weeping in yellow tulips
when the sudden snows come today
been doing a lot of that these days...

From the distance lit signs in the deep dark night in the rolling mountain range of the motor lodges of Vermont appear to read "Jacuzzi, Jesus" be the beacons for the madmen of any real substance and meaning.

Out here you can truly get a taste of the seasons...

Drained with nothing left to say
he asks already knowing--

-Where are you from?

-Nowhere, where you?

-Me too, I'm sure we know
some of the same people...

Starts to think finds it funny how fucken distorted is
American hx how The Civil War started not so much
because of the brutality of slavery but because The South
was threatening to secede from The Union how F.D.R. only
got us involved in the war because Pearl Harbor got bombed
not because of the millions of Jews getting fried in The
Holocaust how such cultural idols and icons who were
originally worshiped and revered such as Lenny Bruce
Jim Morrison and Charlie Chaplin eventually crucified
and excommunicated never to be heard from again
suppose why his best and most keen and profound times
and moments always had been when in transition on-the-run
in a constant state of flux usually from something having to
do with some form of authority or culture with beautiful
divorcees or damaged girls holed-up in fleabag motels
which were like revelations which were like brand new
worlds very much often for such similar-like reasons to
help to gain a whole new perspective which usually was
around that phase or period right before all that damage
and betrayal not too coincidentally somewhere between
The North and South where one can still literally feel
the stirring spirits of those young Civil War soldiers
chilling somewhere right around The Mason Dixon...

On his way out there all he hears over the radio
is static of The Red Sox's (even though he's a
diehard Yankee fan even though it's Spring
Training) as this helps him to plod on and
it always seems to be always eternally seems
to be the state of living always seems to be lingering
somewhere in there in the static of one to nothing...

What to take with you over the border

1. bundle of heroine in sandwich bag
2. cream cheese and raisin bread
3. fresh baked cheddar bread
when zooming through the
heavenly state of Vermont
4. moon pies & lullabies
5. enough change for
tolls & chinese
6. mad libs
7. painkiller
8. jacknife
9. suicide
love letters
10. fresh shoelaces
11. hugs & kisses
12. the smashing pumpkins
13. neil young & janis joplin
14. the short stories of
joyce & dostoevsky
15. reflections & sunsets...

He thinks just want to fall dead asleep head dropping
to the wheel while casually driving at a nice safe speed
completely obeying the speed limit in the middle of the
traffic like some dope addict who just decides to give up
and has had it and that makes just as much perfect sense
to him as anything else right there and then right there
in the middle of nowhere in the middle of the strip mall
with a Denny's & Bickford's & Howard Johnson's & liquor
store right next door to a Laundromat (what could be better
than a liquor store right next door to a Laundromat spending
your whole night your whole life with a nice pint of Mad Dog
in a brown paper bag watching your laundry go round and
round and round with nothing else to do and nowhere else
to go but stagger home) and where ever he ends up ending
up will be just fine and make perfect sense in this futile
brutal and eternal repetitive thing called existence...

A town of souvenirs and old charming brick inns
which romantically allow you to forget and never
remember again solitary chimney swirling from
the slum of the soulful matchstick woods without
a soul around exactly like they like it exactly how
it goes down ravishing naive fast-food girls gruesome
murders which never get spoken about because they're
good people who learn to accept it and just want to get on...

The signs first start reading *Deer Crossing* then *Moose Crossing* and then *Bear Crossing* and then they just say *Moose* and then some silhouette of a reindeer-like creature leaping off to the stars and then the moon and the mountains. When they drop themselves off at *The Northstar Motel* all they can do is trip into the room and fall back back on the big bed and not say a thing and he asks her if she can get him a cold wet towel and put it over his aching head and bloodshot eyes to block it all out, to block out all of life and ask her to arch her back and get on top and ride him naked; This is all you can ever do when taking those long road trips into the deep woods of God's universe way up there into North Country, shower it all off and go back into town for a nice supper as out here it's wonderful and in the windows of the gas stations they got signs up for 6 packs and 12 packs and even 18 packs (and thinks when did they come up with that? And seems so specific and under what circumstances would you need to polish off an 18 pack?) and have a couple while they watch their shows together and then sports muted and love it and forget about it all way up there in no man's land not too far from Canada at the top of the world where the people are much nicer and kinder and just mind their own business and the way it should be; The old night clerk who simply shrugs out of her car hoarding and loaded down with items from her home in the last of the day's sun literally going through the motions from what life has wrought her sneaking into the back screen door to work her graveyard, and you can see by the way she struggles in she has lost so much love, and her image and this simple motion and movement seems like the perfect metaphor for all of existence, and you always got to head back in silence and going back you see those signs again backwards from Bear Crossing to just Moose to Moose Crossing and Deer Crossing and then the image of the big distant illusory city somewhere around where home is and you know you're gonna have to go back there pretty soon...

Thinks about how...

The wife and him spent the weekend up in North Country
and both pretty much hustlers from New York City
and talk to everybody and there was this relatively
young preacher who was lost looking for his flock
looking like he just slept one off while they were
taking their coffee on a bench on the corner
in the beautiful brisk clear air of the morning
after a day of buckets of rain had swept the air
clean and not too many people out on the town
except for the old men smoking pipes over
the river and the bums and the madwomen
and he asked them if they knew where a church was
Methodist one to be more specific because they called
him in to do a substitute sermon and the other pastor
was apparently out sick and told him they were from
out of town but pointed him to a whole mess of them
down the road and he said yeah that's probably the one
looks Methodist and told him just kind of joking around
cause he looked like a pretty nice young down to earth guy
just as lost as himself and who's seen his (fair/unfair) share
of living "As long as you don't have liquor on your breath!"
and just started cracking up while usually is a pretty good judge
of character and he responded in kind "Yeah practice what
you preach, huh?" as seemed as if he'd been around
the block one too many times. Last he saw of him he still
hadn't made it there like some sort of stray dog or hustler
or kid playing hooky and ducking into diners to get his cup
of coffee and hanging out with that tight blue blazer on and
blazing red Irish Catholic cheeks and just strangely kept on
laughing out loud whenever he saw him as seemed like he really
needed it and think always loved people like this who never
ever quite seemed to reach their destiny or calling
or couldn't quite put his finger on it nor really exactly
believe in seemed more con-artists or cartoon characters
and wonder if he ever did make it there to give his sermon
as spiritually and literally was lost and seemed like he sure
as heck could use one himself and sure was a gorgeous
morning in this quaint and charming cobblestone
town of churning rivers and coffee and missing

preachers and bums and mad women on a Sunday
morning in North Country a pleasure running into him...

The eccentric judge who's lost his mind
and now wanders around town with
long white beard and suspenders
like Whitman lagging behind
and all the schmoozers
and wasps and white
collar criminals
from the country
club who some
how got let off
with great
big crooked
smiles going
"Hey judge! How's
the retirement going?"
and him simply nodding
like Buddha forgiving
all that's phony

Hippie girls with their hippie pussies
and hippie beads in bikinis showing
off their hippie bodies with all
the time in the world to kill
and tanning like some strange
surreal dream on the lawn beneath
the great golden dome of the state capitol

Boys trying to keep their high going into third
or fourth day from really good homegrown
tossing frisbees without a care in the world...

Beautiful girl lays out on bench in front of the institution
taking in the sun on a fine Sunday in a small thriving
Vermont town as if paying her dues and taking it all
in no matter what they did to her along the banks
where the river literally over flooded over took
everything with her and where they still got
all those old hotels and factories and movie
theaters seeming that much more ancient
and antiquated and better for the wear
as she simply breathes in and out
the warm summer air becoming
a part of the scene becoming
more aware; no telling
what got her there
but at this point
does any of
that matter?

Sometimes seems like just a hop, skip, and jump
from The Village Idiot, but thinks what's so
bad about it and imagines the benefits...

We fuck so we don't murder
when they literally got knives
coming every which direction

when you're literally searching
for places to hide your fetal position
and got no need to ever come out again

the only thing reliable
take-out Chinese
and the river

an 18-pack
in the window
of the gas station.

Can't sleep because of lucid and vivid nightmares
going all the way back to high school reunions back
to empty cafeterias really feeling like you got no one

swallowed hole by soulless smiling prom queen
waving from her float through the center of
some teaming bleak eternally deserted town

wife getting up like a pop-up penguin in the middle
of the night and offering you her palm of painkillers
washed down with leftover *Crush* by your bed side

motorcycles
taking off to
mountainside.

On your trip home numb
through The Green Mountains
back to idiots and assholes tailing

you through civilization, visions of some postmodern
and devastated overgrown mall filled with leap frogs
and boy sobbing by its side, sophisticated stunning
girl with flat tire on the brink of the apocalypse.

She's young
and solitary
and to die for

You wonder why the aristocrats in very 'exclusive'
and 'desirable' parts of town have always been
the most alienating and biggest assholes and
how in the ghetto they ironically always made

you feel so much more like you belong
(probably because they know what it's like
to survive and suffer just trying to get along)

You wonder the statistic and demographic to all those
who met in those crazy sequined romantic piano lounges
got married how long they lasted and how they ended...

Desperately searching for Chinese somewhere on mad lonely drag strip and heading out of the high-end district and the aristocratic part of town into the sudden deep lonely dusk country and mountains seeing some gorgeous looking young bald headed black man like a beacon with a lovely smile and animated expressions being followed through the big empty rolling hills by this perfect looking spoiled cherubic college girl virgin looking to take victims with blonde hair biting her nails seeming uptight and nervous and what a dichotomy of images and cultures and for some strange absurd reason felt so sleazy and erotic seeing her non-verbals and expressions feeling alienated as hell out here in America searching for Chinese in the middle of nowhere in the midst of this perfectly manicured clean-cut country; When he finally finds it he keeps an eye on his beautiful and cute and adorable wife in the rearview who went in to get menus then comes back out with the food and thinks she's just going to enter and go into the golden doors of that mock emperor's palace and never once come back out again...

He thinks is not practically everything separation-anxiety
and where is that bridge and thing and being and entity
(what's that vision) if anything that can possibly heal it?

Sign simply reads *Ferry To N.Y. State*
along the beautiful banks of the great
majestic and expansive, shimmering
Lake Champlain which just shows up
out of nowhere like some dream like
some sort of miracle over his shoulder
and seems like the perfect escape perfect
stray runaway fugitive route to slip out
in the middle of the evening for junkies
and thieves and delinquents and romantics
and runaways to be redeemed to finally be
left alone again and forgotten within the bleak
blessed brutal and blazing seasons of anonymity...

He thinks he has always been able to relate and learn
so much more has always felt so much more comfortable
around these types of people than any of those domestic
cut-throat creeps who thrive off being judgmental and cruel...

He thinks freedom will never be
having to explain yourself anymore...

Hits the road with son spur of the moment
in squalls of downpour best thing when
needing to get away from it all from all
the goddamn devils on the dead end
America best when enthusiastically
in and out *The Golden Arches* alongside
The Mass Pike of all ages all shapes
and sizes all cultures and everyone
just minding their own business
being cool with each other
'cause all in a state of flux
don't got time to think of it
happily exhausted heading
to long-lost destinations
especially the old timers
and the beautiful young
teenagers with great big
grins gods and goddesses
ready to leap into the rivers
and oceans even being a bit
of a perv looking at the perfect
high school girls sporting those
short shorts flaunting and showing
off those you better not touch milky
white legs for public display always
making their way in *Charlie's Angel* posses
of three all over America the cute country girls
behind the counter with their giggles and whispers
doing their fare share of flirting with him now being
something of a grizzly father boy with big blue eyes
and mop of curly dirty-blonde hair in his soon to be
stained Rocky Balboa t-shirt and mug full of McDonald's
cheese and ketchup and special sauce ending up looking
like some adorable slapstick saintly delinquent clown
and putting one of his stuffed animals into the emptied
out cleaned out carton of fries and big fat stuffed penguin
in sunglasses which from a kid's *Little Prince* perspective
cracked him up and gotta admit cracked dad up also didn't
even have time to get out in those timeless tumbling torrents
not being able to see a thing in front of them with Hogback
Mountain all rapped up in fog and a sweeping firmament
sweeping back to olden times which allowed him to forget

it all all between Bennington and Brattleboro and all those
holy hidden whitewashed inns from Revolutionary War times
which he wishes was in with the great big paper-mache pillars
and buckets of geraniums *guns wanted quilts night crawlers*
a whole flock of turkey vultures who suddenly showed up
out of nowhere washing over windshield and then literally
vanishing into thin air and down into tumbling tragic gorges
just gorgeous infinite and hollow starting to fill up and cause a
commotion but even if they couldn't get out into any of it
at all swear to god all just enough just enough to get by...

Broods...

Today upon feeling a bout of misery and melancholia
Dylan let me nap in his bed in the drizzle and even
put in his nighttime lullabies while he was reading
Dr. Seuss on the rug of his floor and literally had
memories might even call them mild flashbacks
to preschool *Penguilly Day School* to be more
exact which had all these little school houses
with different colored doors red and blue and
green and yellow I once thought for how smart
you were and how smart you weren't right next
door to some great big greenhouse and golf range
and then just started having insane memories of
Junior High School and High School all the wild
and whimsical seasons of wind and snow and rain
and drizzle of old scholar and delinquent friends
and delinquents who usually always were the most
cool and consistent and your first cum fantasies
and pre-cum sexual experiences dirty dancing
dry humping little later on hearing like some sort of
revelation she had a crush on you and you in turn
having a crush on her and getting the guts up to
give her a call with the threat of her older brother
beating you up and when her parents took off to
their very important and formal dinner parties
and her brother to get drunk at keg parties
slipped in and had your first and second
and third and fourth sudden eternal life
changing experience and Dylan walked in
to check on me whispering and asked him
if I could go to my computer and he said no
go back to dreaming we got to get you better...

Will be contented
when they pleasantly
discover his vagabond

bones in the trails
along the side
of the road.

This is his favorite part of the season
when it seems like the butterflies
are falling from the heavens

the tourists picking up their trailers
at the end of summer and leaving returning
the dunes back to pristine Fellini-like desolation

(the cottages
and cafes have
all been evacuated).

When the wilderness chimneys
somewhere set back in the deep forest
start up again with just the feint smell

of blackberry trees
and raspberry bushes
lovers having turned

once again to being
nomadic wanderers
to escape the terrible

routines
and rituals
of civilization

the cider donuts
and maple ice cream
and moon and moose rising...

Today while Dylan invited me to the trails which I so
desperately craved he brought his imaginary friend Clark
with him and told me to bugspray Clark and explained
to me all about the evolution of the world and how it was
painted and when it went dry the people came alive and
strolling with my son through the twilight sun-splashed
trees away from yuppies (that horrible soulless breed of
American) away from the playground so busy trying to act
and judge and one up and be critical and make you feel
like a criminal thought no one could have said it better
and in that moment no one really could how back long
ago somewhere sometime someone painted the world
and when it dried they all came alive and sure as hell
none of these swine and simply able to forgot them all...

Actually tries it himself to have imaginary friends
to see what it would feel like as well and was really
able to feel and get and understand this whole
concept and dynamic made naturally famous
by a kid's imagination for purposes of support
and guidance a bit of object permanence taking on
the form of most necessary forgotten long lost spirits...

Back to demographics & population & median income
& school system: back to the percentages and per capita
ranked and rated in the top 1% of a very competitive and
pristine and puritanical people with the lowest crime rate
and highest rate of graduating future leaders and movers
and shakers; put ignorant and arrogant together, put insular
and all-knowing together and got the Caucasian in America
who self-entitles himself once again with those abstract terms
purposes of attraction and 'selling' them as "family friendly"
and "exclusive" and "desirable" as long as you're the exact
same race and background in a highly 'sought after' part
of town and very 'historical' district which prides itself as
picture perfect postcard of picket fences and paranoia and
prejudice (a collective neuroses which instantly alienates
the 'outsider' and 'stranger' and makes them naturally
'undesirable' and will even make the realty agency
aware of it as well as the town and neighbors, one of
those hidden secret 'understood' codes and customs
in the collective unconscious and conscious America's
become so famous for) and of course their precious
little obnoxious and spoiled children better to be seen
and not heard and treat like extensions and possessions
and eventually turn to fire setting and drug dealing...

Fathers to drinking and
cheating still "trying
to make a name..."

Wives in a daze barreling in a haze
as if in a literal *race against time*
with hair on fire to do errands...

Everyone thrives off a comedy of errors
burying neighbors in gossip and rumors...

He thinks I'm always amazed
at all the people I'm not amazed by
like that breed which always seems to be
desperately trying to make names for themselves...

Always appears something a little more than coincidental
even more than ironic how the supposed 'grownup'
doesn't really quite exactly play by the rules
(just how it will serve their benefit
and best work to their advantage)

Got absolutely no idea what you would call this?

How quickly they turn on you
that's why he always finds
time to beat into the blue
turn to twilight window
when purply pink
pew of sun starts
to explode like
some firmament
from the heavens
helicopters
of America
start to come in
in the beginning
of the season
sports radio
rescues him—
"We got Richie
in Queens
how you
doing?"

The relationship
of the exhibitionist
with the time and weather
with his blinds and shutters
an actual avid true-blue romantic
who for good reason keeps it all in
intimate and from a familiar distance
difference between pedantic and passionate
stuck in the absolutely wrong environment
this is his version of his coping and survival
mechanisms of how he contributes to culture
with specific regulars just as lost and forgotten
here comes teacher whose man walked out on her

Boats and lawn artifacts neatly wrapped in tarpaulin...

Pooh dead
with a happy look on his face
either from an overdose of honey
love making or road kill razorblade
from a rival cartoon character who felt
wasn't getting his just due in 100 Acre Wood...

At dusk he looks up through bloodshot eyes blinds
and finds himself inside a brown paper lunch bag
with a fluff & peanut butter sandwich, a letter
from his mom, a green apple, a switchblade,
bb's, a couple of those old glossy baseball
cards from the early Seventies of all those
losing Mets teams he loved which included
Bud Harrelson, Felix Milan, Ed Kranepool,
Rusty Staub, those bubblegum rock singers
who sang such tragic love songs of loss
couldn't understand at such a young age
and thinks what a weird way for his life
to pass in front of him; There was also
that film they used to play over and over
again in science class about caribou and
all you'd hear from the dark dusty clattering
room from the deep desperate futile blueness
of boredom on some distant tundra repeated
over and over again was *Caribou! Caribou!*

It all comes true and has never left you
from deep within the shadows of this
brown paper lunch bag from school...

He dreams of slicing his
wrists with the ace of spades...

Standing himself up for a blind date...

Loving his wife at knifepoint...

Barbecues go on
and rum added
to the diet cola...

Bugzappers under the constellations...

How all the little monsters get you in the end
somewhere between the stars and superstition...

Garage doors all go down in bat caves together
while garbage cans have been dragged perfectly
to the end of driveways silhouetted like Stonehenge...

Somewhere around the same time every night
the coyotes start up and the wild domestic dogs
musically retort and they go back and forth like some
insane operatic chorus exquisitely crooning their loss...

All that remains is a leftover mitt
and a pair of forgotten binoculars
suspiciously draped over mailbox...

The hallelujah of peepers in the swamp...

Fomite
Burlington, Vermont

Fomite is a literary press whose authors and artists explore the human condition -- political, cultural, personal and historical -- in poetry and prose.

A fomite is a medium capable of transmitting infectious organisms from one individual to another.

"The activity of art is based on the capacity of people to be infected by the feelings of others." Tolstoy, *What is Art?*

AlphaBetaBestiario - Antonello Borra
Animals have always understood that mankind is not fully at home in the world. Bestiaries, hoping to teach, send out warnings. This one, of course, aims at doing the same.

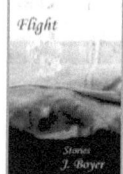

Flight and Other Stories - Jay Boyer
In *Flight and Other Stories*, we're with the fattest woman on earth as she draws her last breaths and her soul ascends toward its final reward. We meet a divorcee who can fly for no more effort than flapping her arms. We follow a middle-aged butler whose love affair with a young woman leads him first to the mysteries of bondage, and then to the pleasures of malice. Story by story, we set foot into worlds so strange as to seem all but surreal, yet everything feels familiar, each moment rings true. And that's when we recognize we're in the hands of one of America's truly original talents.

Improvisational Arguments - Anna Faktorovich
Improvisational Arguments is written in free verse to capture the essence of modern problems and triumphs. The poems clearly relate short, frequently humorous and occasionally tragic, stories about travels to exotic and unusual places, fantastic realms, abnormal jobs, artistic innovations, political objections, and misadventures with love.

Loisaida - Dan Chodorokoff
Catherine, a young anarchist estranged from her parents and squatting in an abandoned building on New York's Lower East Side is fighting with her boyfriend and conflicted about her work on an underground newspaper. After learning of a developer's plans to demolish a community garden, Catherine builds an alliance with a group of Puerto Rican community activists. Together they confront the confluence of politics, money, and real estate that rule Manhattan. All the while she learns important lessons from her great-grandmother's life in the Yiddish anarchist movement that flourished on the Lower East Side at the turn of the century. In this coming of age story, family saga, and tale of urban politics, Dan Chodorkoff explores the "principle of hope", and examines how memory and imagination inform social change.

Fomite
Burlington, Vermont

Still Time - Michael Cocchiarale

Still Time is a collection of twenty-five short and shorter stories exploring tensions that arise in a variety of contemporary relationships: a young boy must deal with the wrath of his out-of-work father; a woman runs into a man twenty years after an awkward sexual encounter; a wife, unable to conceive, imagines her own murder, as well as the reaction of her emotionally distant husband; a soon-to-be tenured English professor tries to come to terms with her husband's shocking return to the religion of his youth; an assembly line worker, married for thirty years, discovers the surprising secret life of his recently hospitalized wife. Whether a few hundred or a few thousand words, these and other stories in the collection depict characters at moments of deep crisis. Some feel powerless, overwhelmed—unable to do much to change the course of their lives. Others rise to the occasion and, for better or for worse, say or do the thing that might transform them for good. Even in stories with the most troubling of endings, there remains the possibility of redemption. For each of the characters, there is still time.

Loosestrife - Greg Delanty

This book is a chronicle of complicity in our modern lives, a witnessing of war and the destruction of our planet. It is also an attempt to adjust the more destructive blueprint myths of our society. Often our cultural memory tells us to keep quiet about the aspects that are most challenging to our ethics, to forget the violations we feel and tremors that keep us distant and numb.

Carts and Other Stories - Zdravka Evtimova

Roots and wings are the key words that best describe the short story collection, *Carts and Other Stories*, by Zdravka Evtimova. The book is emotionally multilayered and memorable because of its internal power, vitality and ability to touch both the heart and your mind. Within its pages, the reader discovers new perspectives true wealth, and learns to see the world with different eyes. The collection lives on the borders of different cultures. *Carts and Other Stories* will take the reader to wild and powerful Bulgarian mountains, to silver rains in Brussels, to German quiet winter streets and to wind bitten crags in Afghanistan. This book lives for those seeking to discover the beauty of the world around them, and will have them appreciating what they have— and perhaps what they have lost as well.

The Listener Aspires to the Condition of Music - Barry Goldensohn

"I know of no other selected poems that selects on one theme, but this one does, charting Goldensohn's career-long attraction to music's performance, consolations and its august, thrilling, scary and clownish charms. Does all art aspire to the condition of music as Pater claimed, exhaling in a swoon toward that one class act? Goldensohn is more aware than the late 19th century of the overtones of such breathing: his poems thoroughly round out those overtones in a poet's lifetime of listening."
John Peck, poet, editor, Fellow of the American Academy of Rome

Fomite
Burlington, Vermont

The Co-Conspirator's Tale - Ron Jacobs

There's a place where love and mistrust are never at peace; where duplicity and deceit are the universal currency. *The Co-Conspirator's Tale* takes place within this nebulous firmament. There are crimes committed by the police in the name of the law. Excess in the name of revolution. The combination leaves death in its wake and the survivors struggling to find justice in a San Francisco Bay Area noir by the author of the underground classic *The Way the Wind Blew: A History of the Weather Underground* and the novel *Short Order Frame Up*.

When You Remember Deir Yassin - R.L Green

When You Remember Deir Yassin is a collection of poems by R. L. Green, an American Jewish writer, on the subject of the occupation and destruction of Palestine. Green comments: "Outspoken Jewish critics of Israeli crimes against humanity have, strangely, been called 'anti-Semitic' as well as the hilariously illogical epithet 'self-hating Jews.' As a Jewish critic of the Israeli government, I have come to accept these accusations as a stamp of approval and a badge of honor, signifying my own fealty to a central element of Jewish identity and ethics: one must be a lover of truth and a friend to the oppressed, and stand with the victims of tyranny, not with the tyrants, despite tribal loyalty or self-advancement. These poems were written as expressions of outrage, and of grief, and to encourage my sisters and brothers of every cultural or national grouping to speak out against injustice, to try to save Palestine, and in so doing, to reclaim for myself my own place as part of the Jewish people." Poems in the original English are accompanied by Arabic and Hebrew translations.

Roadworthy Creature, Roadworthy Craft
- Kate Magill

Words fail but the voice struggles on. The culmination of a decade's worth of performance poetry, *Roadworthy Creature, Roadworthy Craft* is Kate Magill's first full-length publication. In lines that are sinewy yet delicate, Magill's poems explore the terrain where idea and action meet, where bodies and words commingle to form a strange new flesh, a breathing text, an "I" that spirals outward from itself.

The Derivation of Cowboys & Indians - Joseph D. Reich

The Derivation of Cowboys & Indians represents a profound journey, a breakdown of The American Dream from a social, cultural, historical, and spiritual point of view. Reich examines in concise detail the loss of the collective unconscious, commenting on our contemporary post-modern culture with its self-interested excesses, on where and how things all go wrong, and how social/political practice rarely meets its original proclamations and promises. Reich's surreal and self-effacing satire brings this troubling message home. *The Derivations of Cowboys & Indians* is a desperate search and struggle for America's literal, symbolic, and spiritual home.

Fomite

Burlington, Vermont

Zinsky the Obscure - Ilan Mochari

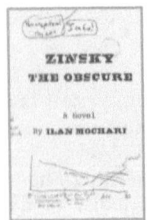

"If your childhood is brutal, your adulthood becomes a daily attempt to recover: a quest for ecstasy and stability in recompense for their early absence." So states the 30-year-old Ariel Zinsky, whose bachelor-like lifestyle belies the torturous youth he is still coming to grips with. As a boy, he struggles with the beatings themselves; as a grownup, he struggles with the world's indifference to them. *Zinsky the Obscure* is his life story, a humorous chronicle of his search for a redemptive ecstasy through sex, an entrepreneurial sports obsession, and finally, the cathartic exercise of writing it all down. Fervently recounting both the comic delights and the frightening horrors of a life in which he feels – always – that he is not like all the rest, Zinsky survives the worst and relishes the best with idiosyncratic style, as his heartbreak turns into self-awareness and his suicidal ideation into self-regard. A vivid evocation of the all-consuming nature of lust and ambition – and the forces that drive them.

Love's Labours - Jack Pulaski

In the four stories and two novellas that comprise *Love's Labors* the protagonists Ben and Laura, discover in their fervid romance and long marriage their interlocking fates, and the histories that preceded their births. They also learned something of the paradox between love and all the things it brings to its beneficiaries: bliss, disaster, duty, tragedy, comedy, the grotesque, and tenderness.

Ben and Laura's story is also the particularly American tale of immigration to a new world. Laura's story begins in Puerto Rico, and Ben's lineage is Russian-Jewish. They meet in City College of New York, a place at least analogous to a melting pot. Laura struggles to rescue her brother from gang life and heroin. She is mother to her younger sister; their mother Consuelo is the financial mainstay of the family and consumed by work. Despite filial obligations, Laura aspires to be a serious painter. Ben writes, cares for and is caught up in the misadventures and surreal stories of his younger schizophrenic brother. Laura is also a story teller as powerful and enchanting as Scheherazade. Ben struggles to survive such riches, and he and Laura endure.

Kasper Planet: Comix and Tragix - Peter Schumann

The British call him Punch, the Italians, Pulchinello, the Russians, Petruchka, the Native Americans, Coyote. These are the figures we may know. But every culture that worships authority will breed a Punch-like, anti-authoritan resister. Yin and yang -- it has to happen. The Germans call him Kasper. Truth-telling and serious pranking are dangerous professions when going up against power. Bradley Manning sits naked in solitary; Julian Assange is pursued by Interpol, Obama's Department of Justice, and Amazon.com. But -- in contrast to merely human faces -- masks and theater can often slip through the bars. Consider our American Kaspers: Charlie Chaplin, Woody Guthrie, Abby Hoffman, the Yes Men -- theater people all, utilizing various forms to seed critique. Their profiles and tactics have evolved along with those of their enemies. Who are the bad guys that call forth the Kaspers? Over the last half century, with his Bread & Puppet Theater, Peter Schumann has been tireless in naming them, excoriating them with Kasperdom....

from Marc Estrin's Foreword to Planet Kasper

Fomite
Burlington, Vermont

Visiting Hours - *Jennider Anne Moses*
Visiting Hours, a novel-in-stories, explores the lives of people not normally met on the page---AIDS patients and those who care for them. Set in Baton Rouge, Louisiana, and written with large and frequent dollops of humor, the book is a profound meditation on faith and love in the face of illness and poverty.

Views Cost Extra - *L.E. Smith*
Views that inspire, that calm, or that terrify – all come at some cost to the viewer. In *Views Cost Extra* you will find a New Jersey high school preppy who wants to inhabit the "perfect" cowboy movie, a rural mailman disgusted with the residents of his town who wants to live with the penguins, an ailing screen writer who strikes a deal with Johnny Cash to reverse an old man's failures, an old man who ponders a young man's suicide attempt, a one-armed blind blues singer who wants to reunite with the car that took her arm on the assembly line -- and more. These stories suggest that we must pay something to live even ordinary lives.

The Empty Notebook Interrogates Itself - Susan Thomas
The Empty Notebook began its life as a very literal metaphor for a few weeks of what the poet thought was writer's block, but was really the struggle of an eccentric persona to take over her working life. It won. And for the next three years everything she wrote came to her in the voice of the Empty Notebook, who, as the notebook began to fill itself, became rather opinionated, changed gender, alternately acted as bully and victim, had many bizarre adventures in exotic locales and developed a somewhat politically-incorrect attitude. It then began to steal the voices and forms of other poets and tried to immortalize itself in various poetry reviews. It is now thrilled to collect itself in one slim volume.

My God, What Have We Done? - Susan Weiss
In a world afflicted with war, toxicity, and hunger, does what we do in our private lives really matter? Fifty years after the creation of the atomic bomb at Los Alamos, newlyweds Pauline and Clifford visit that once-secret city on their honeymoon, compelled by Pauline's fascination with Oppenheimer, the soulful scientist. The two stories emerging from this visit reverberate back and forth between the loneliness of a new mother at home in Boston and the isolation of an entire community dedicated to the development of the bomb. While Pauline struggles with unforeseen challenges of family life, Oppenheimer and his crew reckon with forces beyond all imagining. Finally the years of frantic research on the bomb culminate in a stunning test explosion that echoes a rupture in the couple's marriage. Against the backdrop of a civilization that's out of control, Pauline begins to understand the complex, potentially explosive physics of personal relationships. At once funny and dead serious, *My God, What Have We Done?* sifts through the ruins left by the bomb in search of a more worthy human achievement.

Fomite
Burlington, Vermont

As It Is On Earth - Peter M. Wheelwright
Four centuries after the Reformation Pilgrims sailed up the down-flowing watersheds of New England, Taylor Thatcher, irreverent scion of a fallen family of Maine Puritans, is still caught in the turbulence.

In his errant attempts to escape from history, the young college professor is further unsettled by his growing attraction to Israeli student Miryam Bluehm as he is swept by Time through the "family thing" – from the tangled genetic and religious history of his New England parents to the redemptive birthday secret of Esther Fleur Noire Bishop, the Cajun-Passamaquoddy woman who raised him and his younger half-cousin/half-brother, Bingham.

The landscapes, rivers, and tidal estuaries of Old New England and the Mayan Yucatan are also casualties of history in Thatcher's story of Deep Time and re-discovery of family on Columbus Day at a high-stakes gambling casino, rising in resurrection over the starlit bones of a once-vanquished Pequot Indian Tribe.

Travers' Inferno - *L.E. Smith*
In the 1970's churches began to burn in Burlington, Vermont. If it were arson, no one or no reason could be found to blame. This book suggests arson, but makes no claim to historical realism. It claims, instead, to capture the dizzying 70's zeitgeist of aggressive utopian movements, distrust in authority, escapist alternative life styles, and a bewildered society of onlookers. In the tradition of John Gardner's Sunlight Dialogues, the characters of *Travers' Inferno* are colorful and damaged, sometimes comical, sometimes tragic, looking for meaning through desperate acts. Travers Jones, protagonist, is grounded in the transcendent – philosophy, epilepsy, arson as purification – and mystified by the opposite sex, haunted by an absent father and directed by an uncle with a grudge. He is seduced by a professor's wife and chased by an endearing if ineffective sergeant of police. There are secessionist Quebecois involved in these church burns who are murdering as well as pilfering and burning. There are changing alliances, violent deaths, lovemaking, and a belligerent cat.

Suite for Three Voices - *Derek Furr*
Suite for Three Voices is a dance of prose genres, teeming with intense human life in all its humor and sorrow. A son uncovers the horrors of his father's wartime experience, a hitchhiker in a muumuu guards a mysterious parcel, a young man foresees his brother's brush with death on September 11. A Victorian poetess encounters space aliens and digital archives, a runner hears the voice of a dead friend in the song of an indigo bunting, a teacher seeks wisdom from his students' errors and Neil Young. By frozen waterfalls and neglected graveyards, along highways at noon and rivers at dusk, in the sound of bluegrass, Beethoven, and Emily Dickinson, the essays and fiction in this collection offer moments of vision.

Fomite
Burlington, Vermont

Signed Confessions - *Tom Walker*

Guilt and a desperate need to repent drive the antiheroes in Tom Walker's dark (and often darkly funny) stories:
• A gullible journalist falls for the 40-year-old stripper he profiles in a magazine. • A faithless husband abandons his family and joins a support group for lost souls. • A merciless prosecuting attorney grapples with the suicide of his gay son • An aging misanthrope must make amends to five former victims. • An egoistic naval hero is haunted by apparitions of his dead wife and a mysterious little girl.
The seven tales in *Signed Confessions* measure how far guilty men will go to obtain a forgiveness no one can grant but themselves.

The Good Muslim of Jackson Heights - *Jaysinh Birjépatil*

Jackson Heights in this book is a fictional locale with common features assembled from immigrant-friendly neighborhoods around the world where hardworking honest-to-goodness traders from the Indian subcontinent, rub shoulders with ruthless entrepreneurs, reclusive antique-dealers, homeless nobodies, merchant-princes, lawyers, doctors and IT specialists. But as Siraj and Shabnam, urbane newcomers fleeing religious persecution in their homeland discover there is no escape from the past. Weaving together the personal and the political *The Good Muslim of Jackson Heights* is an ambiguous elegy to a utopian ideal set free from all prejudice.

Meanwell - *Janice Miller Potter*

Meanwell is a twenty-four poem sequence in which a female servant searches for identity and meaning in the shadow of her mistress, poet Anne Bradstreet. Although Meanwell herself is a fiction, someone like her could easily have existed among Bradstreet's known but unnamed domestic servants. Through Meanwell's eyes, Bradstreet emerges as a human figure during The Great Migration of the 1600s, a period in which the Massachusetts Bay Colony was fraught with physical and political dangers. Through Meanwell, the feelings of women, silenced during the midwife Anne Hutchinson's fiery trial before the Puritan ministers, are finally acknowledged. In effect, the poems are about the making of an American rebel. Through her conflicted conscience, we witness Meanwell's transformation from a powerless English waif to a mythic American who ultimately chooses wilderness over the civilization she has experienced.

Did you know that you can write a review on Amazon, Good Reads or Shelfari? Just go to the book page on the website and follow the links for posting a review. Books from independent presses depend on reader to reader communications.

www.ingramcontent.com/pod-product-compliance
Lightning Source LLC
Chambersburg PA
CBHW030257080526
44584CB00012B/349